OF GIANTS and GRIZZLIES

Mary Martin Weyand

Of Giants and Grizzlies

By
Mary Martin Weyand

Copy Editor, Linda Miller Olson, M. A.

Published by Write On For Kids - 2015

See a complete list of all Mary Martin Weyand books which includes all Of Giants and Grizzlies Sequoia 1-10 section titles, newly released eBooks and more at:

http://www.marymartinweyand.com

Copyright ©2015 Write On For Kids,
All Rights Reserved.

No part of this book may be reproduced or transmitted in any form or by any means, electronic or mechanical, including photo-copying, recording, or by any information storage and retrieval system without permission in writing by the author or publisher.

Includes Index:
ISBN-10: 1939060125 ISBN-13: 978-1-939060-12-9

CONTENTS

INTRODUCTION v

DEDICATION vii

SEQUOIA 1. Living Fossils, Giants Of The Forest 1

SEQUOIA 2. The California Grizzly Bear 19

SEQUOIA 3. Black Bears Versus One Tough Wolverine 33

SEQUOIA 4. The Bug-Eating Plant In Huckleberry Meadow 51

SEQUOIA 5. The Pika, A Teensy-Weensy Rabbit 67

SEQUOIA 6. Mysterious Caves Inside The Mountains 79

SEQUOIA 7. The Bird That Walks Underwater 94

SEQUOIA 8. Blazing Topknots 107

SEQUOIA 9. A Circle Of Life 123

SEQUOIA 10. Walter Fry, A Curious Naturalist 139

GLOSSARY 153

RESOURCES 156

MEDIA SOURCES 166

AKNOWLEDGMENTS 175

ABOUT THE AUTHOR 176

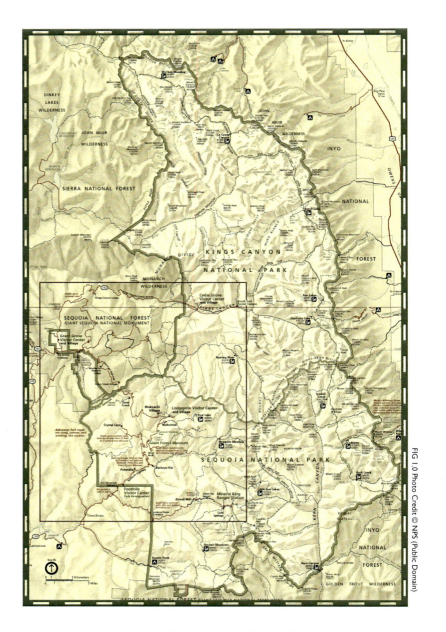

*Sequoia and Kings Canyon National Parks
are located in California's Sierra Nevada.*

iv

INTRODUCTION

"Unimaginable secrets were hidden from newcomers to the vast west of the United States in the late 1800s. Massive trees were the largest and some of the oldest living things on earth. Fearsome grizzly bears, each able to kill a grown man with one swipe of its mighty paw, roamed the land. Innocent-looking plants lured unsuspecting insects to a surprising death, and underground marble caverns with sparkling stalagmites and stalactites kept guard over eyeless creatures that roamed the perpetual dark. These wonders and more were tucked away in the Sierra Nevada of California.

The Native Americans who lived in the West for thousands of years knew about these treasures. But of the new arrivals, only a few were aware of the wide range of wildlife and wild lands that stretched for miles across the tallest mountains in the lower forty-eight states.

In 1890, President Benjamin Harrison signed the law that established Sequoia as the second national park, providing protection from those who would destroy these treasures. At first, the United States Army stood guard when there were no roads and few visitors. Then a man came along who eventually became the first civilian superintendent of the park, and guided it through the early years of exploration and safekeeping.

Walter Fry was first hired to build park roads, and he quickly decided to learn all he could about the mostly unexplored land. He became the park's expert, and was soon named a Park Ranger, then Chief Park Ranger, followed by Superintendent, and finally Park Commissioner.

Walter Wore Many Hats!

While he had changed titles over those forty years, Walter wore the same imaginary hat every one of those days. His make-believe hat could have been labeled "Storyteller." He had many wild animal encounters, experienced spectacular weather events, and traveled through the majestic wilderness. He happily shared the details of these events with others. He was encouraged to record his memories in writing, and he did just that.

Sequoia National Park's "Nature News Notes" was written, typed, and copied by mimeograph over a period of several years. Some of those best stories are shown in italics in each chapter of this book. At the end of each of his stories, you will see - Nature Notes and the date. This is the date that he recorded the event. In each chapter, we learn how the things Walter found and protected are faring in today's crowded world.

Scientific Names of Plants and Animals

If you have pets at your house, you might call them by a particular name. For instance, your dog might be called a name that describes it, like "Shorty," or "Sir Barks-a-lot." Also, your dog has a scientific name (Canis familiarus). The scientific name for your cat is (Felis catus).

Every known living thing on earth is classified and named by a set of rules used by scientists all over the world. Carolus Linnaeus lived in the 1700s in Sweden, and he created this scientific naming system. He used the Latin language to classify living things, including people: (Homo sapiens). In the following chapters, Latin names have often been provided just in case you wish to further learn how the animals and plants of Sequoia National Park fit alongside other living things.

> **Note:**
> As you enjoy Walter's stories, you'll see that he describes animals using anthropomorphic terms (ascribing human characteristics to nonhuman things), which was considered appropriate in his day. Scientists no longer use that kind of language.

DEDICATION

Of Giants and Grizzlies
is dedicated to
the generous spirit of Walter Fry,
who loved and protected
the magnificent and breathtaking
flora and fauna
of Sequoia and
Kings Canyon National Parks.

FIG 1.1 Photo credit © Juan Camilo Bernal

A Giant Tree Hug!

SEQUOIA 1.
Living Fossils,
Giants Of The Forest

FIG I.2 Photo credit © Mary Martin Weyand

There are no other trees like the Giant Sequoias. Millions of years ago they were plentiful and found throughout the earth. In Sequoia and Kings Canyon National Park, they still stand.

FIG I.3 Photo credit © Perri Martin

Smacked By Lightning ~ A Giant Is Cut In Half

❝ *One sunny day in late October 1905, we (myself and a fellow ranger, C. W. Blossom) were headed on horseback down the South Fork Kaweah River canyon from Hockett Meadow to Three Rivers, a distance of twenty-five miles, and a drop downward of almost eight thousand feet. When we were near the 6,500-foot level in the Garfield Grove, to our surprise and amazement we were suddenly confronted with a vast, blue-black, V-shaped cloud, pointing up the canyon. We were just on a level with the top of the cloud and could see both above and beneath it. The cloud appeared to be about three hundred feet in thickness, and in thousands of places the lower current of air was continually breaking upward through the black blanket, giving the appearance of so many miniature volcanoes erupting in succession. Each of these apparent eruptions lasted only a few moments and scattered, in all directions, small fragments of cloud, which soon settled back to the main body. As yet no rain had begun to fall.*

"While we were silently watching this wonderful phenomenon and awaiting the approach of the V point of the cloud, which was moving slowly eastward up the center of the canyon toward us but not touching the canyon walls by some two hundred feet on either side, a tremendous explosion took place on the south side of the pointed cloud about two or three hundred yards from us. Three tongues of lightning darted out. One went up, one down, and one horizontally. This horizontal tongue hit a sequoia about sixteen feet in base diameter and three hundred feet high. The lightning struck over halfway up, cut the tree right in half by knocking out about twenty feet of its trunk, and [split] the remainder in two almost to the ground.

"Never shall I forget that sight. For when the lightning hit the tree, we could see clear daylight through the opening of the cut, and broken chunks of tree scattering everywhere; and while the two split portions of the tree gaped wide apart, the cut-off top of the tree was, for a moment, poised erect in the air above. Only for a moment was this strange spectral treetop suspended in midair. Then it dropped downward between the two open slabs, which clamped tightly upon it. There it is to this day, giving the appearance of a very peculiar tree."

- Walter Fry, Big Trees,
by Walter Fry, John R. White,
Stanford University Press, 1930.

Ancient Giants Among The Dinosaurs

During his forty years in Sequoia and Kings Canyon National Parks, Walter studied the giant sequoia (Sequoiadendron giganteum), learning all he could about its thin seeds, the thick bark, and its huge root system. He thrilled at the knowledge that these huge trees lived millions of years ago. Fossil remains of these trees have been found from the Jurassic period when dinosaurs roamed the earth during the Miocene era, 23.0 to 5.33 million years ago.

Three-toed horses the size of dogs, several types of rhinoceroses, camels, saber-toothed cats, and many other animals lived in North America among the giant sequoia. In those Miocene times, there were no people. Before that, in the Jurassic period there were dinosaurs. The dinosaurs and many ancient animals have gone; the giant sequoias remain.

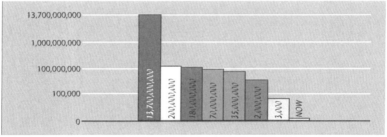

FIG 1.4 Graph Historical Timeline ©CS Martin

Giant trees Time Line - Comparison

- 13,700 million years ago -- Approx. Earth's Birthday
- 200 million years ago -- First trace of Giant Trees
- 180 million years ago -- Dinosaurs appeared on earth -- Giant Trees dominated earth
- 70 million years ago -- Dinosaurs disappeared from earth
- 35 million years ago -- Many volcanoes erupted in the Sierra Nevada
- 2 million years ago -- Sierra Nevada and Sequoia Park landforms began to form
- 3 thousand years ago (estimation) -- The oldest Giant Trees growing today sprouted from seed

Big Trees Around The World

California's mountains are the only place in the world where the big trees remain and grow naturally.

Since the 1850s, scientists from other countries have collected giant sequoia seeds and planted them in their own countries. Big trees now grow in England, Canada, Australia, and many other places around the world.

In the United States, giant trees are growing in Washington, Oregon, the New England states, and other locations. In all these places, the tree seeds have been planted and cared for by people. Those planted trees now growing outside of California are still young, the oldest only 150 years old. They are young compared to the giant trees in Sequoia National Park that are thousands of years old, including the largest tree in the world.

Do You Know?

Giant Trees were here 35 million years ago

Inside Florissant Fossil Beds National Monument in Colorado, visitors can see petrified (converted into stone) stumps of giant sequoias, estimated to have lived approximately 35 million years ago.

An Old Giant!
The General Sherman is the largest tree in the world.

The General Sherman is the largest tree in the world.

Based on its measurements, the General Sherman is estimated to be 3,500 years old. The only way to know the exact age would be to count the rings of the tree.

To understand its height, we could ask sixty-eight children, each four feet tall standing on the head of another. That would make one giant tower of children almost 272 feet high, the height of the General Sherman. To figure its width, you could take seven average, medium-sized cars and place them side-by-side. The General Sherman would still be wider, at thirty-seven feet wide.

How heavy is it? Add up the weight of 391 male elephants or 716 female elephants to equal the weight of the General Sherman Tree. Its total weight is estimated at 4,299,851 pounds, or 2,145 tons. That's a lot of tree!

Seeds Of The Big Trees

Big trees are so huge that you might wonder, "How big is the seed that becomes a giant tree?"

A brand new giant sequoia sprouts only from seed. The cones that grow on the tree contain the seeds. Unlike pine trees you might have in your yard, the giant sequoia cones are very small. They are about the size of a golf ball. The petal-like parts of the cone are called scales and each scale holds three to eight seeds at its base.

FIG I.6 Photo credit © Mary Martin Weyand

Big tree seeds are less than a quarter of an inch in length. The actual seed rests between two "wings," as Walter describes. There are seventy-four seeds resting on this teaspoon.

Walter Watches The Seeds Scatter

It is a wonderful sight in the forest on a bright autumn day when the seeds are falling - this of Nature sowing and distributing the seed over the forest floor. The seeds are very light, over three thousand to the ounce, and a very slight breeze carries them far away, each seed volplaning on its thin, stiff wings. Every little rustle of the branches pours down seeds in great volume, looking like thousands of golden insects as they slide off through the air."

- Walter Fry, Nature Notes

In the spring, soon after the snow has melted, tiny plants burst from the fallen seeds and push up tender green leaves. The seeds grow successfully in mineral soils, in full sunlight, free of other vegetation. But a sprouting seed that might be a giant tree someday may become a quick meal when it sprouts.

Birds, such as sparrows and finches, are attracted to the plants and pick off the topmost portion for food. Cutworms destroy many of the seedlings by cutting them off near the ground to eat them. Large black wood ants chop off the fresh tops and drag the greenery to their nests. Ground squirrels and chipmunks also eat the tender tops. Many of the seeds take root in places where the soil is either too wet or too dry, and they soon perish. Only a few seeds live to produce young trees.

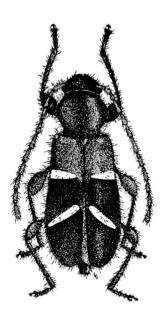

The Longhorn Beetle

A Seed Here - A Seed There

Though many insects and small animals can be found in the trees, two in particular help the giant sequoia distribute their seeds.

The "babies" of the Longhorn Beetle (Phymatodes nitidus) look like caterpillars or worms, called larvae. They bore into the pinecone. Cones invaded by the beetle larvae during the summer will slowly open over the next several months, allowing the seeds to fall. While it appears that the beetle is damaging the cone, it actually helps to release the seed. Likewise, when the Douglas squirrel (Tamiasciurus douglasii) gnaws on the pinecone, some seeds are dislodged and drop to the forest floor where they will sprout.

FIG 1.8 Photo credit © Daniel Smith

The Douglas squirrel gnaws on giant sequoia cones. Some seeds are dislodged and dropped to the forest floor where they will sprout.

Inside The Tree

Sap circulates throughout a tree's vascular system, and can be thought of as something like the blood that circulates throughout the human body. It delivers nutrients, like vitamins, that are stored during winter. In the growing season, the roots take up water and minerals. These mix with nutrients to feed the tree's growth. When the giant tree is wounded, the sap oozes out and forms a glossy skin. Like a bandage, the sap protects the tree while it heals.

When young, the tree has a small taproot (a central root). To this taproot, lateral roots are attached by the hundreds, leading off in all directions. Eventually the taproot disappears. The roots of a mature giant tree spread over an area of between two and three acres. That's bigger than two football fields!

The Tree's Skin

You might think that the bark of such a big old tree would be hard and tough, but instead, it is soft. You can almost stick your finger into it. Up to two feet thick, the spongy bark is perfectly designed for repelling flames. The big trees live for thousands of years, and they experience many fires, most started by lightning. The pine trees, the firs, and the cedar trees die in the flames. The big tree, however, lives through fire after fire.

Walter Fry Had Two Tests Conducted So He Could Learn More About The Bark

"*On August 25, 1899, a slab of bark 18 inches in diameter, 2 feet broad, and 6 feet long was placed in the furnace of the Atwell sawmill, surrounded by dry pine, and the whole set on fire. When the fire had died down it was found that, although the pine had burned to ashes, the sequoia bark remained practically unharmed, except that it was, of course, charred on the surface.*

On September 6, 1907, Mr. A.J. Robertson, superintendent of the Mount Whitney Power Company, attempted to force 5,000 volts of electricity through a piece of bark one inch square and five inches long, but without success. The tests show the resistance of the bark to fire and electricity."

- Walter Fry, Nature Notes

Do You Know?

Giant Sequoias grow their own bandages.

- Little by little, about half an inch a year, new bark creeps over a fire scar, so in time, it will repair itself.

Fire Among The Trees

In the early 1900s, people responsible for the park believed that fire severely threatened the trees, and fire was avoided. Great effort was made to put out all forest fires.

Later, as the trees were studied, it was found that fire is necessary to the good health of the giant trees. Fire clears the ground so new seeds can germinate. Ash from the fire protects fallen seeds from getting a sunburn (ultraviolet radiation).

A controlled burn is set by professional firefighters when wind and weather conditions are good. This is done to safely reduce the vegetation from beneath the giant trees.

Damaged Roots

People camped on the roots and next to gigantic trunks many years ago. Damage was done to the roots by people digging into the ground around the tree (for instance to pound in tent stakes). Beginning in 1950, the park service developed new rules, and people were no longer allowed to camp under the trees or drive cars on top of the roots.

OF GIANTS AND GRIZZLIES

FIG. 1.10 Photo credit © Perri Martin

I once found a hibernating bear soundly sleeping in that fire-scarred hole,"
said Walter Fry. " . . . In the spring he departed from his sleeping spot."

MARY MARTIN WEYAND

FIG. 1.11 Photo credit © Perri Martin

Deadwood at the top of the General Grant Tree has been there for hundreds of years. When large fires encircle the giant trees, sap may be prevented from reaching the top branches, causing them to die.

In 1929, tractors were used in the park and driven over tree roots. Today, care is taken by forest personnel to protect the roots.

During Walter's time, up until the 1940s, nearly 300 buildings were built in the Giant Forest, including cabins, motel units, gift shops, a gas station, and more. A recent study showed that the presence of all those buildings put stress on the root systems of the giant trees. As of December 2009, almost all of the buildings have been removed. Thousands of native trees and plants have been planted in the ancient grove.

"The Giant Forest restoration improved the experience of seeing the trees, which is sort of the heart of what this park is all about," said retired Sequoia and Kings Canyon Chief Naturalist Bill Tweed.

Athena Demetry, Restoration Ecologist with the National Park Service adds, "Along with the demolition came the opportunity to allow fire to do its work. Dozens of young sequoia trees sprang up in the aftermath of a now ten-year-old burn of the forest. Other areas of the grove, without young sequoias for years, have seen a similar rebound." Walter would be thrilled with this restoration.

In Summary

Sequoia 1. The Giant Trees - Then and Now

✓ The big trees in Sequoia and Kings Canyon National Parks are no longer cut down. From 1890, the giant trees have been protected.

✓ Beetles and squirrels distribute pinecones and help the release of seeds.

✓ From 1950 to 1960, changes were made to prevent both camping underneath the big trees and driving on their roots.

✓ As of 2009, the Giant Forest area has been restored. Almost 300 buildings have been removed, improving the long-term needs of the root systems.

✓ The cleansing use of fire has been returned.

✓ New giant sequoia trees are sprouting in the forest.

A grizzly bear takes a breath. Is it snorkeling or catching salmon?

SEQUOIA 2.
The California Grizzly Bear

> *Prior to the arrival of white men in California, the California grizzly bear had practically nothing to fear or disturb his peace and happiness. True, once in a great while the Indians succeeded in killing a grizzly, but such instances were very rare ... The grizzly had no other animal to dread as an enemy, for as a fighter he was a master of all."*
>
> - Walter Fry, Nature Notes, November 4, 1924

In the 1800s, and many hundreds of years before that, grizzly bears (Ursus arctos californicus) roamed the entire state of California, including the area designated as the Sequoia National Park. An abundance of food was available for the bear's daily feast: huckleberries and wild plum, trees laden with nuts, tule roots and truffles, and vast fields of clover. The bear stole honey from the bees and snatched deer and elk kills from mountain lions. The great grizzly bear could easily eat his fill undisturbed, satisfying his thousand-pound girth. Rarely did he encounter trouble. That is, until the white man showed up. Though a measly size compared to the great bruin, man carried a deadly firearm. Filled with fear and dreadful stories, the armed man was quick to shoot and kill.

OF GIANTS AND GRIZZLIES

The Native People And The Grizzly Bear

For many hundreds of years, long before the white man came, the Native American tribes that made California their home greatly feared the grizzly bear. In 1860, Hupa children and an elderly woman came upon a grizzly, and this story is told:

When she was a small child, Susan Little of the Hupa Indian tribe, along with some playmates, was gathering hazelnuts in the company of an elderly woman. Suddenly, they heard bear sounds in the bushes. The children, not being afraid of the black bears, knew nothing of the grizzly. They wanted to sneak up on the animal and frighten it away with sharp yells. But the old woman, when she saw the bear, ordered them to freeze in their tracks. "Stand like sticks," she said quietly.

Susan remembered the beast as "a great big brown with a great red mouth and big red eyes." The animal was tearing up a thicket of hazel bushes. The children were so terrified that they wanted to run, but the old woman kept them still, even for a long time after the grizzly had gone. -Recounted in 1952 by Susan Little to Robert Talmadge.

Mikyowe (Me-cha-e-s)

- The Hupa called grizzlies Mikyow or Mikyowe (Me-cha-e-s), which means "great big browns" in the Hupa language. This distinguishes them from "little blacks and browns," the same kind of bears that we see in the Sequoia today.

Even before that time in the late 1700s, grizzlies were killed by Spaniards with muskets. But it was white people who entered the state in large numbers and the search for gold that spelled doom for the grizzly. Many stories are told of encounters between a grizzly bear and a gun-toting man. Some happened in the area of Sequoia National Park.

On November 5, 1906, Walter Fry visited Joseph Palmer, who lived along the Kaweah River, near the town of Three Rivers, the gateway to Sequoia National Park. He told Walter of his experience with a large grizzly bear.

In The Dark Of Night
1865-Joseph Palmer's Story

In November of 1865, I was asleep in my cabin on the south fork of the Kaweah River, when the squealing of my hog woke me. He was in a six-foot-high log pen about fifty feet away. It was quite dark outside. Even so, I grabbed my rifle and ran out in my nightclothes. I leapt over into the hog pen. Just then I saw a large dark animal reared up in front of me with the hog in its mouth. It was attempting to climb out of the pen.

"I jabbed the muzzle of my rifle against the animal and fired. It fell over backwards against me and caused me to fall. The bawling bear and squealing hog were almost on top of me. Never in my life was I so badly scared. After gaining my feet, I hopped over the six-feet-high logs in one jump and ran to my cabin where I stayed for the rest of the night. I didn't sleep anymore.

"When I went out in the morning, I was greatly surprised to find that it was a grizzly that I killed. My pig was dead as well. When I weighed the grizzly, I found out that the male weighed nine hundred and sixty-seven pounds."

- Walter Fry, Nature Notes, November 4, 1924

OF GIANTS AND GRIZZLIES

*On their hind legs, bears can reach eight to ten feet tall.
How tall are you?*

Just like the hungry bruin that killed the pig, all California grizzlies were erased by men like Joseph Palmer. Even though Mr. Palmer intended no specific harm to the bears, his cabin was built in an area where these great bears had lived for thousands of year.

Bear by bear, grizzlies were killed until only a few of the estimated 10,000 remained. In the book, California Grizzly, the authors say that there was active hunting of grizzlies in California before the gold rush, but the greatest reduction (in numbers of grizzlies killed) was probably between 1849 and 1870 . . . the bears were killed not only for their meat but also to prevent them from injuring the settlers and killing livestock.

August 7, 1921 - Grizzly Sighting

Many years later, on August 7, 1921, eleven park visitors saw a large gray bear at the Giant Forest "bear pit", a place where bears ate garbage thrown away by people. It was practically twice the size of other adult black bears. This particular bear had a distinct hump at the top of its shoulders, a sure sign that this was a grizzly. They reported that as the animal appeared, other bears ran hastily away.

A few years later, during the month of April 1924, Mr. James B. Small and his road-working crew of several men reported on more than one occasion having seen a large, grizzly colored bear near Moro Rock. All of the crew made mention of the hump at the bear's shoulders.

On October 13, 1924, Mr. Alfred Hengst, a cattleman of Three Rivers, came into very close contact with a huge bear near the headwaters of Cliff Creek. Hengst said, "It was the biggest bear I ever saw - bigger than my cow, and looked as though sprinkled over with snow. Undoubtedly, it was a grizzly."

During this same year, several different people, at different times, spotted bear tracks that were over twelve inches in length and six inches wide. Such tracks are much larger than those made by black bears.

Many thought that all of these sightings were of one and the same grizzly.

OF GIANTS AND GRIZZLIES

Finally, an official warning was posted:

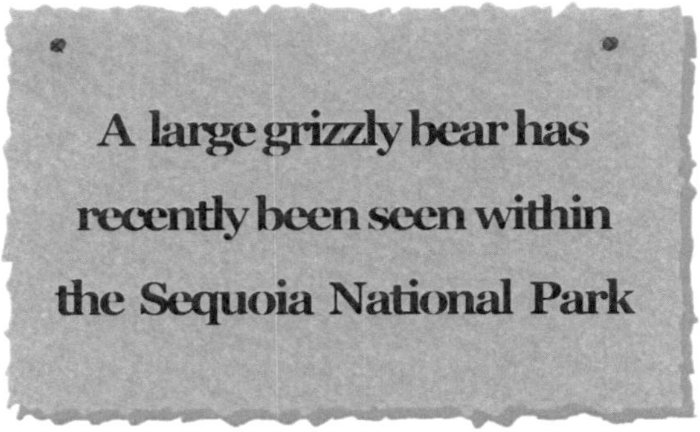

A large grizzly bear has recently been seen within the Sequoia National Park

FIG 2.3 Graphic News Clip © CS Martin

> 66 *The tracks as well as many reports let us know that this was for sure grizzly country. I felt pleased that as long as the great bear was in the park, it would be protected."*
>
> *- Walter Fry, Nature Notes, November 4, 1924*

Gone From California Forever

After these many sightings in 1924, that great California grizzly bear was never seen again. Its fate unknown, it appears to be the last California grizzly ever reported.

The extinction of the California grizzly was motivated by fear of these awe-inspiring animals. Ferocious when defending itself or protecting its cubs, grizzly bears are known to keep a distance between themselves and people. The grizzly might still be in California if people had recognized that these great bears needed space to live. This recognition has happened in Montana.

Today, Rick Bass, a naturalist and celebrated nature writer, lives in grizzly country in Montana, where the great bears still thrive. In 1996, he wrote the foreword for the book California Grizzly by Tracy I. Storer and Lloyd P. Tevis Jr., saying, "Each small thing we discover about these incredible animals raises two new questions, questions we didn't even previously know how to ask . . . [like the importance of] the bear's role in seed dispersal . . . [we see that] all things are connected. The grizzly likes to live in untouched, unharmed areas - in places of mystery . . . places in ever-diminishing supply on the public lands of the West these days." Further he says, "The very least we can do is commit these last places -any wild and good country - to the future, as wilderness reserves . . ."

Montana, Where Grizzlies Still Roam

Karl Rappold owns a 17,000-acre ranch in Montana, and his family has owned it for 130 years. The land looks very much the same as when Lewis and Clark were exploring the American West beginning in 1804.

For a quarter-century, one of the biggest grizzlies in the lower forty-eight states has lived on the Rappold ranch. "The only thing I do to live with that great bear is to keep cows out of the upper pasture (the one nearer the bear den) when the 1,000-pound grizzly comes out of hibernation," Rappold says.

Not only are grizzlies in Montana, but also Wyoming, in and near Yellowstone National Park, and in northern Idaho; and they are still abundant in Alaska.

Is It A Grizzly?

By traveling to the places where they still live, you might be lucky enough to spot a grizzly bear in the wild. When you look through your binoculars, you'll wonder, "Am I looking at a black bear or a grizzly?"

If you see a bear but are not sure that it is a grizzly, you will know by its shoulder hump, also seen on young cubs. Its hump is a large mass of muscle that helps it to dig for nutritious roots. The grizzly fur has a shaggy look, with various shades of color, unlike a black bear whose coat is one solid color.

OF GIANTS AND GRIZZLIES

*The shoulder hump and varied-colored coat separate
brown grizzly bear from the black bear.*

 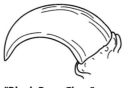

"Grizzly Claw"   "Black Bear Claw"

Grizzly claws are longer, broader, and heavier than those of the black bear.

Twice as large as black bears, male grizzlies weigh from six hundred to one thousand pounds. The females weigh less, between three hundred and five hundred pounds. Grizzly claws are longer, broader, and heavier than those of the black bear. Grizzlies use their long front claws to dig for bulbs, roots, and rodents, as well as for fighting.

Without grizzly bears, black bears rule!

❂ The absence of California grizzly bears provided an opportunity for black bears to expand their range. Black bears are now found throughout the state of California.

Grizzly Banquets

Grizzlies eat almost anything and everything. They are known to eat whale carcasses, field mice, bees and grubs, berries of all kind, deer and elk carrion, gophers, wild plums, wild cherries, lizards, grasses, truffles, frogs, nuts, roots, fish, and acorns. Fresh out of their winter dens, a dozen or more grizzlies can be seen in meadows at the same time, digging for bulbs or munching on fields of clover. They eat spring flowers, rose hips, aspen tree tips, the bark of alder trees, aspen and cottonwood trees, grasshoppers, and so much more. One time, a bear was known to eat about a hundred pounds of potatoes from a garden. Almost everything, it seems, is food for the grizzly.

As meat eaters, grizzlies only occasionally kill large animals, but they get much of their meat meals as carrion - the flesh of dead animals. No grizzly in California has been known to eat human flesh.

Where the Grizzly Sleeps

When a grizzly creates a new den, it does so by digging out large amounts of dirt, or it will start with a natural cave, making it larger. The entrance hole is three or four feet around and six to ten feet deep. A larger space is rounded out at the back and is used for sleeping. Its entire floor is thickly carpeted with leaves and grass, with only one adult bear for each den.

Newborn Size - Scoop of Ice Cream

Sows (adult female bear) use dens when they give birth to bear cubs, usually in January. Mother's milk keeps the small cubs well-fed.

At birth, they weigh less than one pound (usually eight to twelve ounces) and about the size of an ice cream cone. They have fine, short hair, but appear hairless. After forty days, they weigh two pounds, and their eyes are open. They remain in the den with the mother bear until spring.

Young cubs are fed mother's milk.

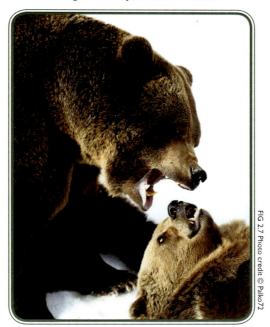

"You pay attention to me!" Is that what she is saying?

A Threatened Species

In 1975, the grizzly bear was listed as a threatened species under the Endangered Species Act. They were protected until 2007 when they were taken off the endangered list, due to the improved numbers of grizzlies. When this happened, it only took a few years for the number of grizzlies to begin to decline again. As of 2009, the grizzly bear has been returned to endangered-species status. It is threatened by the decline in food provided by the white bark pine tree, a tree that is increasingly destroyed by the mountain pine beetle. The seeds from this tree are a key food for the bears, particularly sows, as they prepare for winter each year.

Added to this threat is the illegal killing of the grizzly bear by hunters, even today. Park rangers and game wardens in the northern United States work to save the grizzlies by arresting those who harm them.

The Endangered Species Act

✳ The Endangered Species Act of 1973 is a law that protects plant and animal life at risk of becoming extinct and disappearing forever. This law helps people find ways to improve conditions for at-risk plants, animals, and their ecosystem.

California Grizzly Is Gone

No more can we gaze in awe at the huge grizzly bear in the California mountains. "Lost forever" is a phrase that eats away the joy found in the discovery of a huge paw print, or the sight of the great bear lounging in a berry patch. There is still time to recover the grizzly bear in the places where it still lives.

Do You Know?

The California Flag

- In 1911, California adopted the grizzly bear as the state's emblem.

FIG 2.8 Illus. credit © Devin Cook

In Summary

Sequoia 2. The Grizzly Bear - Then and Now

- ✓ The grizzly bear that roamed Sequoia National Park in Walter's day is one of the last grizzlies recorded in California. There are no more California grizzly bears.
- ✓ Grizzly bears still exist in Alaska, Idaho, Montana, and Wyoming states.
- ✓ Today, many people respect all animals, including predators. In the past, most people believed that predators should be killed.
- ✓ The grizzly is listed as threatened and is protected by the Endangered Species Act. However, in places where they still live, some grizzly bears are still killed by people every year.

Ready for a food fight!

SEQUOIA 3.
Black Bears Versus One Tough Wolverine

Traveling deep into the forest on horseback, Walter often camped for several days or even weeks at a time. He was careful to keep a journal of events that happened. In the following true telling of what he saw, we get a glimpse into the animal world when only a few people were there to see what happened.

Black Bears Meet Their Match

It was on the evening of June 20, 1906, with United States troopers . . . in Sequoia National Park, I established camp for the night in Buck Canyon at an elevation of 7,800 feet. Our camp was located beside a beautiful mountain stream in the center of a green meadow, by rough broken country of red fir forest and brush thickets. It was the best game region of the park. We saw many deer, bear and other species.

"Scarcely had we made camp when we heard the growlings and mutterings of bear. In order to locate the disturbance, we walked out on a nearby precipice. Reaching the edge of the cliff, we saw below us a small grassy opening, some 150 feet away. There in plain sight were two large bears, one a black and the other a brown, standing on the decomposed carcass of a cow.

The animals were disputing over the right of possession, but after much growling, they both squatted side-by-side in friendly, if malodorous repast.

"*Undetected, we watched the bear for some fifteen minutes. Then we saw a large wolverine emerge from some brush about one hundred yards to the rear and above the two bears. The wolverine seemed to have nothing in particular on his mind, but was just walking, ambling along at a slow walk with an occasional glance to either side.*

"*Whether the wolverine was returning from a long, unsuccessful hunting trip in an effort to obtain food, or was just starting out for his evening hunt, was not certain. But, I am of the opinion [it was] of the former, for the animal showed signs of being both fatigued and hungry. He first lay down for a few minutes; then got [up and] turned over a good-sized log under which he found a few snails, which he ate. Next he walked a few paces to a large fir tree, from the base of which he jerked a large fungus and swallowed it with one gulp. Then he directed his attention to catching and eating frogs from some puddles of water.*

"*The wolverine continued on his frog hunt for a few minutes only. A sudden shifting of the wind brought to his nostrils the scent of carrion [that] wafted on the breeze up the canyon. At this he sprang on top of a large boulder, pointed his nose, locked in the direction of the scent and espied the two bears. He watched them for a few moments, eyeing the space between him and them, stood for a short while studying in a thoughtful mood, then slid quietly to the ground and sat down. He hung his head in serious meditation as if trying to reason out the best possible method to obtain possession of the carcass. Soon his bristling hairs told of his decision. It was fight to death if need be, but have the carcass, he must.*

"Shifting his position a few paces to the right, he secured protection of a large boulder within thirty feet of the bears, which shielded him from their sight. Advancing continuously but quickly to the boulder, behind its shelter, he brought his passions of anger to full height and preparation, ready for the affray. He stood up rigid, peered around one side of the boulder, his passionate anger glittering in his bead-like eyes, while the hair on his back and neck was erect and rough like that on a dog when going into a fight. His short, brushy tail (sic)was hoisted to an almost perpendicular angle. Then, after having bristled himself up to what appeared double his natural size, in this queer and picturesque attitude, the wolverine shot down the mountainside, landed directly on top of the carcass between the two bears, and ferociously growled and snapped his powerful jaws and teeth in their very faces.

"Never in all my mountain experience have I seen wild animals more suddenly and thoroughly frightened, than when those two bear looked up and saw the wolverine so close and in such a hostile attitude. Every combative impulse gave way to hysterical fright. The brown bear gave three enormous bounds and landed high on the side of a large fir, to the top of which he climbed. His companion turned a complete summersault (sic)backwards, and landed on his feet, head foremost downhill; and he departed at such speed that only a cloud of dust drifting towards the western horizon marked his course.

> ❝ Then the wolverine began devouring the carcass in an effort to satisfy his ever gluttonous appetite; but when one of the boys of our party approached him, he gave a coarse growl, grabbed a large bone in his mouth, and walked slowly into the depths of a cherry thicket. Whereupon, the brown bear came down the tree and ran away.
>
> "Never have I been able to figure out why the bear were so outrageously frightened at the onslaught of the wolverine; unless they had been taught by long experience that the wolverine is an animal that once engaged in combat, fights to the death."
>
> - Walter Fry, Nature Notes, July 30, 1906

Black bears climb trees to get away from trouble.

Even when resting, the wolverine displays his mighty paws and claws

Wolverine, A Fierce And Solitary Predator

Compared to a black bear (Ursus americanus) that weighs hundreds of pounds, the wolverine (Gulo gulo) is about the size of an average family dog, weighing about twenty-four to forty pounds. The wolverine is powerfully built, with strong jaw muscles and large, heavy teeth. It can easily eat frozen meat and bone. Its claws are long and sharp. The wolverine's diet is primarily meat, usually consumed as carrion (already dead animals). Occasionally it eats eggs, wasp larvae, berries and other forest food, as well as live animals.

Are Wolverines Still In Sequoia Park?

The number of wolverines that remain in the Sequoia and Kings Canyon National Parks is unknown, as few have been spotted in recent years. There may be several reasons for this.

While thick fur keeps it comfortable in the coldest weather, the wolverine may find the now warmer California weather too hot. After all, it can't take off its heavy coat!

In addition, the wolverine builds its den in snow areas at or above the tree line where there are few people. Human activities such as cross-country skiing or the building of a road might cause wolverines to escape to more remote areas. When it travels, it does so alone over territory that stretches for hundreds of miles, making it difficult for scientists to track.

Surprisingly, in March 2008, a wolverine's picture was taken by a motion and heat-detecting camera in the Sierra Nevada Mountains, north of Sequoia Park. There is hope that the wolverine is still with us in the Sequoia and Kings Canyon National Parks.

Black Bears Are Not Only Black!

As you drive on the park road, you might get lucky and spot a bear as it ambles across the paved highway in its constant search for food. The name "black bear" is misleading, as they come in many colors, including blonde, cinnamon, and brown. All are members of the same species.

Full-grown boars (male bears) weigh approximately 300 to 350 pounds, and sows (female bears) weigh about 100 to 250 pounds. Black bears have a narrow head and powerful limbs, and can run at speeds of up to twenty-five miles per hour for short distances. They also climb and swim with agility.

This bear was feeding on acorns, yet quickly picked up speed to cross the road.

Though they have small ears, they have better hearing than humans and are able to hear high-pitched noises, just like dogs. Black bears see poorly, yet have the ability to distinguish color.

Daniel Gammons, the Wildlife Biologist for Sequoia and Kings Canyon National Parks says, "Bears experience their environment primarily through their noses - it is the main way they obtain information about the location of food, potential mates, and potential predators. They would make great bloodhound dogs, if they were not so ornery!"

Black bears have a long, flexible tongue that can bend and grasp food, and teeth adapted for feeding on both plant and animal matter. They have five toes and long claws on both front and hind feet.

Where, Oh Where, Is The Black Bear?

Walter was located in a meadow at 7,800 feet when he spied the bears in his story. They are mostly found in the park's mountainous terrain above 3,000 feet where thick vegetation and seasonal fruits, berries, and nut crops grow. Availability of trees in their habitat is important to bears. Not only do they eat the seeds and nuts, but they quickly climb the trees to escape predators. When winter comes, a rotted fir tree or a hollowed-out tree trunk is sometimes utilized for a winter den.

Though the exact number is unknown, some estimate that there are hundreds of black bears in the 850,000 acres of Sequoia and Kings Canyon National Parks. While they can't keep track of all bears, Sequoia Park biologists monitor selected bears to determine their health, eating habits, and contact with humans.

A Park Full Of People

When Walter first traveled through Sequoia Park, the black bears kept their distance, moving away as he approached. People and bears had little interaction at that time because few people ventured into mountainous terrain. Then roads were built, and more and more people used the parks. The availability of human food became an "easy" meal for hungry bears. The bears quickly discovered the park garbage dump and would gather there each day to eat the disposed food.

People recognized that the dump was a great place to see bears, and came to watch. As a result, bears found an easy way to be fed. Bears that scavenged human food frightened people, and park rangers realized that a mistake had been made. The garbage dump was removed in 1940, but some bears continue to identify human food as bear food.

Way too close! Bears came daily to Bear Hill, a place where bears gathered at the garbage dump, and people came to watch. It was finally closed in 1940.

*Terrific noses pick up any food smell.
Even a single stick of gum can result in a bear break-in.*

The odor of human food draws bears like a magnet. Terrific noses pick up any food smell. Even a single stick of gum can result in a bear break-in. Every year, some hikers return to their car to find the car door torn off and the seats ripped to shreds by a bear. The bear might have smelled something as small as a candy wrapper or hand lotion that smells like food. Today, rangers warn visitors to rid their cars of all traces of food when parking.

Daniel Gammons, wildlife biologist, and fellow bear technicians team up in the summer months in Sequoia to discourage "campground bears" that like to raid human food under the cover of darkness. In their natural state, bears search for food during the day. By contrast, bears drawn to high-calorie human food have learned to hunt at night when people are less apt to confront them. Gammons patrols highly visited areas, watching and listening for any sign of the bears. Barking dogs and people making noise often alert the bear patrol members, and they hurry to the spot. Besides their voices, patrols use a 12-gauge shotgun that uses nonlethal rubber slugs to drive the bears away. "Some of these bears have been shot before. All they need to hear is the sound of that shell loading and they're gone," Gammons said. "Unfortunately," he added, "they are usually only gone for a short period of time. We can change their unwanted behavior in the short-term, but it is almost impossible to make a bear want to permanently forage on natural foods once it has had a taste of high-calorie human foods."

Finding food is natural for the bears, even if it's in a paper wrapper. It is people who must be more careful in bear country. A bear that eats human food learns to approach people and their cars and houses. Because this is a threat to humans, the bear may end up having to be destroyed. That's why rangers say "A Fed Bear is a Dead Bear."

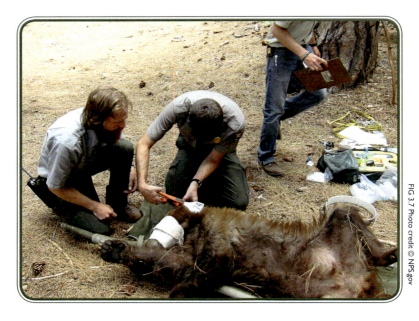

FIG 3.7 Photo credit © NPS.gov

Danny Gammons, National Park Service Wildlife Biologist, keeps a sharp eye while Michael Saxton affixes an ear tag to a young female bear.

Even Bears Have Tattoos!

If a Sequoia bear has a habit of checking out camping areas for people food, a VHF radio-telemetry collar might be fitted on the bear. This is accomplished by loading a drug in a special dart gun, then shooting the dart into the bear. The drug temporarily knocks out coordination and blurs its senses. While it's sedated, park rangers attach the collar, place a numbered tag in its ear, and tattoo the lip of the bear for permanent identification.

A numbered tag allows park personnel to identify a bear from a distance. But the tag and the collar can be lost from the bear, so a lip tattoo is used in case the bear is found without other identification. Also, while the bear is sedated, blood samples are taken to check its health.

This five-hundred-pound, male black bear has very big paws! Green ink on the person's hands is from tattooing the bear's lip with permanent ink.

FIG 3.8 Photo credit © NPS.gov

The primary use of the telemetry tracking information is to intercept a bear before it gets into a developed area. Rangers try to prevent bears from getting human food in the first place, rather than reacting to an incident after it has already occurred. Eventually, the collar drops off a bear's neck and is retrieved by a ranger.

Gammons is happy to report, "Between 1999 and 2008 we've shown a sharp decline in the number of bear-to-human run-ins. It's down 62 percent, and property damage by bears is down 81 percent. This is much better for the bears."

OF GIANTS AND GRIZZLIES

Bears Make Signs

- People mark trails with informational signs for other people to see. Bears also leave their marks in the forest. They leave messages that other bears can "read." You can watch for their telltale signs.

Bears make their own marks on trees.

Clawed Trees, Big Footprints

Claw marks and bites: Bears claw and bite trees to leave the message that they were there. Bites leave nearly horizontal scars that look like a dot and a dash where the upper and lower long, pointed (canine) teeth come together. Sometimes, a strand of the bear's fur gets caught in the bark when it is marking a tree. Bite marks are usually from 5 and one half to 6 and one half feet high on a tree or pole.

Rubbing against objects: Black bears of all ages rub their scent to mark trees, as well as wooden signposts and utility poles. They rub their shoulders, neck, and crown in order to leave their scent as a message to other bears.

Bear scat: Watch for bear scat (feces). Sometimes bear scat is intentionally left by bears to communicate information about themselves to other bears. You might have seen dogs smell the feces left by other dogs and cats. While humans think this is gross, it is an important way animals use to deliver information.

For example, the smell of droppings and urine might tell a bear whether they are near a female with cubs, a large male, or a not-yet-grown yearling. A young male might want to stay away from a large adult bear, but want to find and join another young male bear as a companion.

FIG 3.10 Photo credit © Kim Cabrera

Bear feces shows evidence of the food that bear has been eating.

When walking on trails, watch for bear paw prints!

Paw prints: Unlike humans, a bear's large toe is on the outside of the foot, and the smaller inner toe doesn't always show in the bear print. Bears often follow deer trails and forest roads. In fact, some trails are used mainly by bears. These trails consist of a series of depressions created by multiple bears placing their feet in the same footsteps year after year. Bears have been known to use a stiff-legged walk; by pushing their paws firmly in the soil, they seem to be emphasizing the news that they've been there.

Rangers tell people to stay on marked trails to limit erosion and damage to the area. A bear that hears humans nearby will move away from the noise. This is why you should make noise when hiking through the park.

Bears Are Eating Machines

Black bears seem to have a good memory for the location of food and the time of year when that food can be eaten.

Like people, they are omnivores, eating both meat and plants. A bear is an opportunistic eater that feasts on grasses, roots, berries, fish, fungi, moss, mice, marmots, ground squirrels, bird eggs, cereal crops, cattle, sheep, and the young of deer. It even eats insects, tearing into the nests of ants, bees, and termites and their grubs. It will also eat carrion when it's available, as in Walter's story about the bears and the wolverine.

When a black bear emerges from its den during March each year, it spends a lot of time eating fresh meadow plants. It's amazing how a bear can tear up a meadow as it digs roots out of the ground, leaving upended clods of dirt. Meadows are very important sources of food in the spring and summer months. For example, Round Meadow in Sequoia National Park may have as many as twelve bears feeding at one time.

Black bears especially like acorns, pine nuts, and the seeds of the sugar pine tree. They have been spotted shaking oak trees to dislodge acorns. One day in October 2008, Sequoia Park Service Botanist Sylvia Haultain observed a large female bear lying down under a blue oak tree. The sow was shoveling a large quantity of ripe acorns into her mouth. Rich in protein, the acorns add needed fat for winter hibernation. "She was pretty busy with her food, so I left her undisturbed," Sylvia commented.

Bears Are Clever

How smart are bears? Bear biologists who've measured bears' intelligence say that the average black bear is smarter than a German shepherd, widely regarded as one of the smartest dogs. Bears have the heaviest brains, relative to body length, of any carnivore.

Bill Lea, wildlife photographer, took a picture of a bear as it moved a log into place over water. It then walked across the log to get to the other side of the creek without swimming. Although bears can swim, this bear apparently wasn't interested in a swim on that particular day. This is an example of an animal using a tool to accomplish a task-an ability normally accredited to humans and chimpanzees.

A Place To Sleep

When winter comes, black bears tend to hibernate. They will stay in their den and mostly sleep while the snow gets deep and the nights grow long. During hibernation, their body temperature reduces to 88 degrees. Their warm fur allows them to retain body heat, and they live off of their own fat. Each adult bear has its own den site. If the Sequoia Park winter is warmer than usual, some bears may leave the den during winter to look for food.

Fig 3.12 Photo credit © Mark Bertram, FWS

Newborn cubs removed from a tranquilized mother, still in her den. They are tagged, weighed, and returned unharmed.

Black bear dens are found in a dry spot, protected from rain and snow. Dens are located in caves, in slash piles (cut or broken tree limbs), under large rocks, or at the base of rotted or fire-damaged trees. Sows make a bed out of sticks, grasses, and leaves, and they give birth during hibernation.

Sequoia 3. The Black Bears And Wolverines - Then and Now

- ✓ Fewer wolverines are seen now. Possibly, a warmer climate and the increased number of people in the parks have affected the wolverines.
- ✓ More is known about bears today than in Walter's day. Selected bears are collared so that bear specialists can monitor their health and understand how they use their habitat.
- ✓ People are not allowed to have food where bears can get it. The garbage feeding of bears stopped in the 1940s. Continued efforts to control the availability of human food has resulted in fewer bear-and-people "run-ins."
- ✓ The black bears are as plentiful in the Sequoia and Kings Canyon National Parks as they were in Walter's time.

Fig 4.1 Photo credit © Scaners3D

Let me go!, Let me go!

SEQUOIA 4.
The Bug-Eating Plant
In Huckleberry Meadow

A fly, looking for a tasty meal lands on a dewdrop. Instantly its tiny feet are stuck as if in glue, a captive of the sundew. The innocent-looking red hairs close on the fly, holding it tight. The more the fly struggles, the more entangled it becomes, until it dies. The best way to find a sundew plant (Drosera rotundifolia) is to look for a stem that is topped by small white or pink flowers above round, pad-like leaves that lie flat on the ground. Use a magnifying glass to look closely at the leaves. They have numerous hairs, one-half inch or less in length and reddish in color. On the ends of the hair, fluid is formed. The fluid glistens like a dewdrop. (You'll get the idea by thinking of how a tear forms in the corner of your eye.)

The sundew plant gets needed minerals and vitamins from the insects it captures. It seems to have rules about the capture of insects. For instance, if a very small insect lands on a leaf, just a few of the tentacle-like red hairs close over the bug to capture it. But if a fairly large insect lands on the sundew, all of the hairs quickly close over it. Each leaf has its special work to perform and works independently from the others. After the digestible substance has been extracted from the insect, the hairs rise to their former, upright position. As they rise, the undigested particles of the last capture rise with them, to be carried away by the wind. The sundew is now ready for its next victim.

Huckleberry, A Wet Meadow

Each spring when the weather warmed, Walter rode his horse to Huckleberry Meadow and stayed for days at a time. By then, the sun had melted the wintertime snow and created the wet meadow once more. Walter didn't walk through the meadow, because it's soaked mud, tender plants, and small animals' homes could easily be trampled and ruined. It was his favorite place to take in bird sounds, animal chirps, and the sweet fragrances of colorful flowers. He loved to pause and watch the carnivorous plant, found along the meadow's edges.

The Sundew Plant - An Experiment!

66 *On June 29, 1908, while camped at Huckleberry Meadow, I decided to conduct experiments covering a period of 30 days, by feeding certain [sundew] plants on various sorts of food, different from their regular diet. For the experiment 6 plants that stood close together in the patch were selected. They were all vigorous plants, of about the same size, in heavy leafy stage, containing 10 leaves each, and no leaves bore evidence of having yet captured insects. All plants were given their first food during the noon hour, and every leaf was given as large a morsel of food as it was capable of handling. So there were 60 little traps all set for action, and which closed upon the food as fast as it was given. All plants were given special kinds of food thereafter as fast as they could digest it. The following foods were given, and results obtained:*

- *Plant Number 1. Fed fat salt bacon: [The sundew] was dead by morning of July 3. One feed given.*
- *Plant Number 2. Fed on California cheese: was dead by the evening of July 9. One feed given.*

- *Plant Number 3. Fed on ordinary house-flies: lived the period throughout, ran up flowering stock 7 inches high, containing 8 flowers; also fertile seed. Four feeds given.*
- *Plant Number 4. Fed on wood ants: lived the period throughout; ran up flowering stock two and one half inches high, which was dead by the 23rd of July without flowering. Two feeds given.*
- *Plant Number 5. Fed on Mountain ladybug beetles: lived the period throughout but never went beyond the leafy stage, and looked quite puny at the close of the test. One feed given, upon which the plant worked all the while excreting digestive juices in an effort to decompose what nitrogenous material the beetles contained, rendering it available for the nourishment of the plant without apparent result. All beetles were practically whole at the close of the test, and tentacles [of the sundew] were clasped tightly over them.*
- *Plant Number 6. Fed on fresh beef's liver: lived the period throughout, ran up a flowering stock 14 inches high, containing 29 flowers; also contained good, fertile seed. Both, flowers and seedpods, as well as the leaves, were unusually large. Five feeds were given.*

"All insects were killed by method of pin puncture prior to their being fed to the plants; as this was necessary for the reason that traps were not strong enough to hold them when given alive. Only one insect at a time was given to each leaf.

"One day a hungry yellow jacket [wasp] lit on a plant leaf and attempted to steal one of the liver baits; but one bite was sufficient to satisfy his taste, for he left without taking it and had some difficulty in extricating two of his feet from the trap . . . I hope this most interesting plant lasts for many years to come."

- Walter Fry, Nature Notes, June 29, 1908

OF GIANTS AND GRIZZLIES

It's an ingredient for medicine.

- The sundew is a plant known around the world. In the twelfth century, an Italian doctor by the name of Matthaeus Platearius described it as an herbal remedy for coughs. Today, it is used in cough medicine for the treatment of lung-related illness, and in medicines for other purposes. Farmers grow the plants and sell them to medicine manufacturers.

The Huckleberry Bush

Along with the sundew plant, a type of huckleberry shrub called the "western blueberry," (Vaccinium uliginosum), is plentiful. The meadow was named after this low-growing plant.

In the spring, look for its small, pale pink flowers shaped like upside-down vases. Dark blue berries replace the flowers, and ripen in July and August. In the heat of summer, black bears show up to munch on this delicious treat, as do a variety of birds including the yellow-rumped warbler (Dendroica coronata).

Bears and birds compete for the delicious huckleberry fruit in summertime.

Yellow-rumped Warblers gobble up insects as well as berries.

In 1906 and again in 1931, Walter produced a survey of birds in the park. He noted that the yellow-rumped warblers were as plentiful in 1931 as they were in 1906. Just as he could, you can often hear the warbler's call, a sharp 'tsip' sound.

As large numbers of these birds gather, their song, a mellow, tinkling, (turly urly, urly, urly, urly, i-ci) echoes through the forest. Their cheerful summer feathers, a mix of yellow, charcoal grey, black, and white are brighter than their winter coat. The birds dart out beyond the leaves and circle back to the tree. When you see this looping behavior over and over, you'll know they're catching an insect each time.

Corn lily plants signal the arrival of spring.

Another good place to spot warblers is among corn lilies (Veratrum californicum) in the wettest part of the meadow. As you stay off the wet meadow and far from the birds, your binoculars will come in handy. You can watch the birds pick off aphids for a tasty meal. Corn lilies are usually the first to poke through melting snow in spring and get their name from the flowers that look like the tops of cornstalks.

MARY MARTIN WEYAND

FIG 4.5 Photo credit © Walter Siegmund

The Sierra shootingstar reminds us of fireworks.

Ever Seen A Shootingstar?

Growing among the corn lilies and other meadow flowers is the Sierra shootingstar (Dodecatheon jeffreyi). The flower's pink-to-crimson petals bend backward and appear as if the flower is about to dive off its long stem. Among the many spring flowers, you'll often notice bumblebees nearby.

Dive Bombers On A Mission

Has a black-and-yellow, striped bumblebee (Bombus pennsylvanicus) ever zipped past your ear, making a high-pitched, intense buzz? If so, you probably jumped. They seem scary. They're loud and noticeable, but they don't sting humans unless threatened or bothered.

The bumblebee sounds scary, but isn't.

These busy bees pollinate flowers, including the Sierra shootingstar. The bumblebee grasps the anther (the part of the stamen where pollen is produced) with its legs or mouthparts and shakes its flight muscles rapidly without moving its wings. This motion shakes electrostatically charged pollen (it's like dust or powder) out of the anthers. The pollen is attracted to the bumblebee's oppositely charged body hairs. Carrying the pollen it has gathered, the bumblebee flies to a different Sierra shootingstar and repeats the process. As a result, the flowers are pollinated and will reproduce.

Do You Know?

Returning bees carry food on their legs.

- It seems a silly thought to imagine yourself carrying a sandwich strapped to your legs! Carrying food is what a bumblebee does. It grooms any remaining pollen from its body onto its back legs for transport, and delivers the pollen to be fed to developing bees.

Cautious gopher emerges from its tunnel to stuff its cheek pockets with food.

Meadow Grasses, A Great Hiding Place!

Across a wet meadow floor, many kinds of grasses, and grass-like rushes, and sedges grow. You are probably used to seeing grasses that are mowed, but in the meadow, grasses grow tall. What hides on the floor of the wet meadow among the greenery?

Sit quietly overlooking the meadow, and you might see a furry head pop out of its burrow in the grasses. The mountain pocket gopher (Thomomys monticola) will dart out quickly to snip pieces from the green plants. It carries its food back to its burrow using special pockets that extend from its cheeks to its shoulders. The pockets are lined with fur and can be turned inside out and then put back again using a special muscle. It hurries its food gathering to avoid many predators, including foxes, weasels, owls, and skunks. It uses its large front teeth to clip grasses, and its long fore-claws to dig dirt. The gopher helps the meadow stay healthy by continually loosening the soil as it makes tunnels and nesting chambers.

Ripples move across the surface of the meadow's water. Look closely, because the disturbed water could be caused by a Sierra gartersnake (Thamnophis couchii). Pale gray with dark checkering on top, its belly is salmon-colored, often heavily marked with black. The Sierra gartersnake swims by looping its body sidewise, and can move fast across grassy areas, as well as in the water.

Dinner for this nonpoisonous snake is fish, amphibians (frogs, toads, and salamanders), and water insects. Unlike other garter snakes, the Sierra gartersnake is not known to eat mice. It hunts during the day, even underwater, where it can find an abundance of its favorite foods, such as the frog.

Before you see it, you'll hear the very tiny Pacific treefrog (Hyla regilla). While only three-quarters of an inch to two inches long, it can make BIG sounds! In water, and sometimes from hidden places on land, the male inflates his throat pouch and utters a loud kreck-ek at one-second intervals. He continues to call for long periods of time. If many frogs are calling all at once, you might have to hold your ears!

"In your face!" this garter snake seems to say.

The song of the tree frog can be heard in many Hollywood-made movies.

The frogs are brownish to olive green, with dark spots that are pale in the center. They actually don't spend much time in trees, but you might see them hiding in rock crevices, under bark, or on stream-side vegetation.

Females lay loose clusters of up to seventy eggs attached to underwater plants or sticks in shallow water. Tadpoles hatch from the eggs, then grow and change into frogs. The song of the tree frog can be heard in many Hollywood-made movies.

While frogs must be alert to becoming a snack for a snake, they are quick to snatch spiders, ants, flies, and a variety of insects for their own dinner, including mosquitoes.

Life stages of a Mosquito

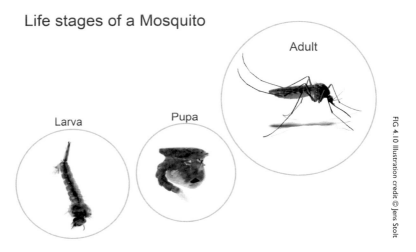

FIG 4.10 Illustration credit © Jens Stolt

Mosquitoes become food for many birds, frogs, snakes and more.

Slap! Slap! Slap! That's the sound you might make as you swat away mosquitoes (Anopheles freeborni). That is, unless you've used an environmentally safe bug repellent, or wear protective clothing. Pesky mosquitoes bother coyotes, birds, rodents, and many other warm-blooded mammals, including people.

Mosquitoes lay eggs on or near water. Tiny, wiggly larvae hatch from the eggs and begin feeding on decaying plant matter. Larvae develop into pupae that change into adults. The adult mosquito flies in search of a warm-blooded mammal (watch out, it could be you) to have a blood meal. That is, unless it is intercepted by a frog, a bat, or a dragonfly.

MARY MARTIN WEYAND

Very, very fast, the dragonflies capabilities may influence the design of small robotic flying devices. These clever flying insects have had considerable time to become good at what they do.

4.11 Photo credit © John A. Anderson

When you see a dragonfly, it sees you no matter where you are.

They've been around for three hundred million years, long before the dinosaurs.

If you visit the meadow in late summer, you might see large numbers of the Common Green Darner Dragonfly (Anax junius) as they swarm before migrating south for the winter.

The mosquito, busy looking for a blood meal, might not see the dragonfly coming as it zips across the wet meadow at high speed, clocked in one case at thirty-six miles per hour. When you see a dragonfly, it sees you no matter where you are. Dragonfly eyes have about 30,000 lenses and can see all the way around, except directly behind themselves. (Can you imagine being able to see in all directions at once?) The dragonfly uses the basket formed by its legs to catch insects while flying. Whether a gnat, a mayfly, a fly or a mosquito, insects do not have a chance of out-flying a dragonfly. Instead, they become lunch.

Life Feeds Life

The balance of nature can be seen in the meadow. The air and the water join with the already rich soil to nurture the plants and trees. Tiny creatures use the soil and the plants as they crawl and fly about the forest area. Small and large creatures enjoy the fruit and seeds supplied by the trees, shrubs, and grasses. Smaller creatures are eaten by larger creatures. Animal droppings and dead carcasses add nutrients to the meadow and forest floor and, in turn, enrich the soil once more. Far from being yucky mud, the wet meadow earth is the foundation of the forest, a combination of mineral particles from rock, water, air, and organic matter. It was formed and recycled and maintained over many thousands of years. There are many more plants, insects, and animals in Huckleberry Meadow than we've enjoyed so far. Like Walter Fry, you can discover them.

In Summary

Sequoia 4. The Sundew Plant And Huckleberry Meadow - Then and Now

- ✓ The sundew plant still catches insects in Huckleberry Meadow.
- ✓ The sundew plant continues to be used to make cough syrups and other medicines.
- ✓ Bears still dig roots and eat berries.
- ✓ Birds, bats, frogs, and dragonflies can be seen eating gnats, flies, and mosquitoes.
- ✓ Bumblebees still pollinate flowers.
- ✓ Gophers and mice loosen meadow soil, as they did in Walter's day.

Pika carries a treasure to its haystack

SEQUOIA 5.
The Pika, A Teensy-Weensy Rabbit

> *Pikas (Ochotona princeps) appear to be a family of [mammals] that has come down through the ages* as a survival of the fittest to live in a region difficult for other animals to utilize. . . . The presence of pikas was first noted in the Twin Lakes basin on July 15, 1906. They had recently taken up residence in a huge rock slide, which had rolled down the steep mountainside to the east during the previous winter. The colony at first consisted of five animals; it has rapidly increased and ranks as one of the largest in the Sierras."*
>
> - Walter Fry, Nature Notes, August 24, 1922
>
> *The high hills are a refuge for the wild goats; and the rocks for the conies [rock rabbits or pikas] - Psalm 104:18, The Bible

Do You Know?

An artist's view

- Some believe that the inspiration for Pikachu, the popular Japanese Pokémon character is the pika. This might be true as there are pikas in Japan.

Extra-warm In A Cold Spot

The pika's normal body temperature is 104.0 degrees Fahrenheit, compared to a human's normal temperature of 98.6 degrees Fahrenheit. It has adapted to live in a cold climate. In fact, if it overheats in its thick, furry pelt, it can die in minutes. This means that it must remain high in the mountains or dwell only in cool places.

Humans Nearby! "Eeek-Eeek"

Hikers who reach high-altitude rock taluses often hear the pika's call before they see it. But that's not always true. Some encounters are quieter. Naturalist Guide, Linda Wallace tells of her first experience with a pika:

"On a backpacking trip in the eastern Sierra Nevada, I was sitting on the talus rocks that descended into a lake [this was most likely the same spot that Walter described]. I was taking in the magnificent scenery when I felt something on the top of my foot," she says. "I looked down to see a small, furry creature, the color of my dusty sneaker. It was a pika! My shoe blended with the color of the rocks," Linda continues, "and the pika sat quite comfortably on my foot for several minutes as both of us gazed out over the lake. Eventually, it scampered off, leaving me with the feeling that I'd been welcomed into this piece of wilderness that I was experiencing for the first time."

FIG 5.1a Photo credit © Ben Kucinski

Mount Whitney is the tallest mountain in the lower 48 states at 14,505 feet.

FIG 5.2 Illustration credit © Carol Heyer

Artist's painting depicts shoelace encounters, rendering by Carol Heyer

Biologist Chris Ray shares a different shoe story about the pika: Chris tells of one day when she sat patiently near a pika's den, waiting for it to come out of hiding. "I may have been there for more than a half-hour, just staring at rocks. I felt and heard something at my feet. Surprisingly, it was the pika I was waiting to see, tugging on my shoelace. I believe it was trying to take the lace to its hay pile! I laughed to think I was looking all around, and this little creature was right next to me. I study the same groups of pikas year after year," Chris explains. She sets out mesh traps concealed with rocks. When a pika enters the trap, Chris reaches inside and tags one ear with a color-coded tag. The animal is released, and can then be identified throughout its lifetime.

Do You Know?

Hiking up to 10,000-foot altitude is hard work, but rewarding.

- Hiking up a mountain is hard work. People might become breathless and panting as they climb higher and higher. This is because the air at higher elevations has less oxygen compared to the air near sea level, where most people live.

- The view is spectacular, like the view from an airplane window. While hiking, it's possible to see Mount Whitney, the highest peak in the lower forty-eight states. Mount Whitney is 14,505 feet high and located within Sequoia National Park.

- Camping at high altitudes is great for stargazing. Streetlights are actually a kind of pollution. You will be surprised by the wonderful sea of stars when looking into the sky from 10,000 feet.

> ## Swim-challenged
>
> *The pikas have a horror of getting into deep water."*
>
> *- Walter Fry, Nature Notes, August 24, 1922*

By following the rocks to a lake, pikas can obtain a drink during the winter without being seen by predators. However, they don't like to jump in! In an emergency, they will swim for about fifty or sixty feet, but that's their limit.

A Mountain-high Rocky Home

The pika doesn't create a den. Instead, it makes its home among the rocks. It stays in the area where it was born. For instance, the Twin Lakes area has had pikas living there for over one hundred years. With a lifespan of three to four years, many generations have lived on the same rock-strewn talus area.

Cold Air Versus Hot Air!

Only something alarming like a shortage of food, or crowded living conditions, cause pikas to leave their chosen talus area. In order to find a new home, they might have to travel to the top of the next mountain. To do that, they have to go down their mountain, cross over land at a lower elevation, and go up the next mountain. If the air temperature at that lower elevation is much hotter, the pikas could overheat, causing sickness or death. For this reason, scientists worry that pikas are stuck on their mountaintops just as people might be stuck on an island in the middle of an ocean.

The Endangered Species Act

In 2003, a study found that six of twenty-five high-elevation pika groups have disappeared. The authors of the study think that this loss is due to global warming. After more research in May 2009, the U.S. Fish and Wildlife Service announced that pikas were the first mammal considered for protection under the Endangered Species Act. As of December, 2011, this protection has not been provided.

Sidenote: Global Warming

The earth is showing many signs of worldwide climate change. The average temperatures have climbed 1.4 degrees Fahrenheit around the world since 1880.

Fig 5.3 Photo credit © Carly Lesser and Art Drauglis

Busy pika carries an abundance of treasure to its haystack.

Little Hay-Makers

66 *In some places they are called Conies, and in others Little Chief Hares. Here in the Sequoia National Park they are called the "Haymakers of the Sierras" because of their food-gathering ways."*

- Walter Fry, Nature Notes, August 24, 1922

People gather hay and oats and store it for their cows and horses. In much the same way, pikas gather flowers and grasses into "hay piles" to store food that is eaten throughout the snowy winter. They rely on nearby grasses and wildflowers for a steady food supply.

Pikas eat a large variety of green plants, including different kinds of grasses, sedges, thistles, and fireweed. Sedges differ from grasses by having solid stems. Thistle is a prickly plant. Fireweed is a flowering plant that has purple or pink blooms and lives as high as thirteen thousand feet.

These little "rock rabbits" use their strong teeth to cut the stems, and then carry their hay to rocks and boulders within their territory. They move or turn the pile several times a day to keep it in direct sunlight so that it dries out. It is a busy time.

While a pika is out foraging, its nearby pika neighbor might try to raid its hay pile. Owners who catch the robber in the act chase it away.

In winter, the haystacks of food are protected by the snow, which acts as a winter blanket. It holds heat from the ground and protects pikas and their food from icy storms. During winter months, pikas also find mosses and lichens to eat by traveling in tunnels they've made under the snow. Lichen is a fungus that grows on the surfaces of rocks, trees, or soil. In the mountain talus areas, many kinds of lichen provide both food and nesting material.

Watch Out For Enemies!

One summer, scientist Chris Ray and her four assistants were gathered on a talus patch. A pika stood on rocks above the group, calling "Eeek-Eeek!" The pika came closer and called again. "We didn't move, but watched to see what it would do," Chris explained. The pika came closer. An assistant was sitting on some rocks, and that little pika ran up to him and bit him on the thumb! It didn't break the skin. He said it was like a pinch. "We all admired the little animal for its bravery among us much larger humans," Chris said.

Pikas can bound quickly from rock to rock. They've been seen leaping distances of ten feet or more when closely pursued by an enemy.

Weasels, (Mustela erminea), are the pika's prime enemy. They are quick to attack, and they use their strong claws to catch and hold their prey. Weasels are carnivores that eat only meat, and they must eat frequently to maintain good health. Pikas recognize the musky smell of the weasel and hide in a flash when weasels are nearby.

Clever weasel stands on hind legs to search for a pika.

Red-tailed hawk enjoys a meal (a marsh rat, not a pika)

The red-tailed hawk, (Buteo jamaicensis) is another enemy to watch out for. As he flies overhead, pikas utter sharp sounds to signal danger. All nearby pikas scurry to their hiding spots to avoid the cruel talons of this swift-flying enemy.

Newborns To Adults In One Summer

Usually, four or five pika youngsters are born at once in the spring. For the first ten days, their eyes are shut and they have little hair. They grow rapidly, reaching full size in two months. The mother cares for them until about the seventh week when each is weaned and left to care for itself.

OF GIANTS AND GRIZZLIES

FIG 5.6 Photo credit © Mark Byzewski

When caught out in the open, it is sometimes wise to sit absolutely still and pretend like you are a rock.

> ❝ *The weaning is hastened by the mother's running away from the young upon their approach and hiding among the rocks. After only a few months of life, the young leave the nest area to find their own territory."*
>
> *- Walter Fry, Nature Notes, August 24, 1922*

In Summary

Sequoia 5. The Sequoia Pika - Then and Now

- ✓ Climates, warmer today than in Walter's day, have caused pikas to move to even higher elevations to stay cool.
- ✓ A warming climate affects the amount of rain and snow each year. The changing weather may cause an abundance or decline in the nearby food supply.
- ✓ Because the pika is temperature-sensitive, a continuing increase in average air temperatures could threaten their presence in the park.
- ✓ The pika may become protected by the Endangered Species Act.

FIG 6.1 Photo credit © Dave Bunnell

SEQUOIA
6

Trained Junior Caver, Colin Prest, experiences a day of caving.

SEQUOIA 6.
Mysterious Caves Inside The Mountains

American Indians who had lived in the Sierra Nevada for thousands of years knew of the caves. However, the discovery of a large cave on the western-facing side of the Sierra Nevada surprised the recent arrivals. Little did they know that there were many more caves to be found. Since Walter's time, and year after year, new caves are found. Athletic cavers (people who explore caves), often scientific-minded, squeeze their way through tight places and endure cold temperatures in order to experience the spectacular caves.

> ### The Discovery Of Crystal Cave
> ### Beauty Hides In The Dark
>
> *Cassius Webster and Alex Medley had the same two days off from their hard job of constructing park trails. With a packed lunch and their fishing poles, they headed for nearby Sierra streams on an April weekend in 1918.*

> *"Looking up from his fishing spot along Cascade Creek, Medley saw a dark opening behind some bushes. The men hiked closer and felt a cool breeze. They decided to investigate. To their surprise, hidden behind the bushes lay a tremendous cave entrance. It was 10 feet tall and 30 feet wide with a large passage that headed straight back into the mountain! After walking a short distance inside, they hurried back to camp and reported their discovery."*

FIG 6.2 Photo courtesy © Perri Martin

Cascade Creek still tumbles down the mountain near the Crystal Cave entrance where the men were fishing.

"Two days later, along with others, Walter Fry arrived at the cave. Inside there were long tunnels. On that first day they made it through the tunnels as far as a room now named the Junction Room.

"On many more days, the men explored the cave, and found eight separate circular rooms. Some were larger than others. The rooms were from 40 to over 100 feet wide, and from 20 to 60 feet high. Walter decided that the best name for this beautiful place was "Crystal Cave."

"It is in this cave that nature had lavishly traced her design in decorative glory. Throughout the entire cave, the stalactite formations are ornate and vary by size, form, and color. In some of the rooms the ceiling is a mass of stalactites, some very large, others tapering down to needle points. Others drop down from the roof's great folds of massive draperies. In some chambers, pipe-like columns of stalagmites reach up from the cave floor.

"The beauties of Crystal Cave have not been damaged. The National Park Service has kept the cave closed ever since the discovery. As of this writing in 1925, we are hoping the Congress will supply the money to install adequate lighting. Until the caves are developed, park visitors are forbidden to enter without special permission from the Superintendent's office."

- Walter Fry, Nature Notes, June 20, 1925

The Caves Formed Long Ago

Walter and others returned a few days later to go deeper into Crystal Cave. Not sure of what they would find, they slung ropes across their shoulders and held lamps high and bravely ventured farther into the darkness. This was the first cave discovered by the National Park Service after Sequoia National Park was named.

Walter and his group found tunnels, irregular passages, and even large caverns formed by slowly moving groundwater that dissolved the limestone and marble over many thousands of years. You can think of the cave as a part of a huge, underground plumbing system carved out by water.

Inside Crystal Cave, formations are created by water and minerals.

In Sequoia and Kings Canyon National Parks, many caves have been found along the western side of the mountains. There are other caves throughout the world, but few contain marble walls as these do. While Crystal Cave was not the first to be discovered, it also wasn't the last.

Crystal Cave Since Its Discovery

Starting in 1938, workmen labored to build a road to a spot where they then added a steep walking trail to the cave entrance. The men blasted passages open with dynamite, using the smallest charges possible to avoid breaking cave structures.

On May 29, 1940, Crystal Cave was opened to the public. This was in the last year of Walter's life, and surely he liked knowing that park visitors would be able to enjoy Crystal Cave for years to come.

Some 80 years later, Walter's great-great-great grandchildren, Quinn & Caden Martin prepare to enter the Spider Gate entrance to Crystal Cave. The clever design lets cave critters come and go, yet protects the cave when closed to visitors

Over three million visitors have walked through the cave since 1940. Almost all of them have been careful to avoid damaging the cave. Unfortunately, a few people broke off pieces of the delicate cave features for souvenirs. Today, tours are restricted to small groups that can be safely guided by park rangers to stop further damage.

Discoveries are still possible in Crystal Cave. In 1999, a new deep-blue underground lake was found there. Most cavers call it Crystal Blue Persuasion, after a pop song from 1969. Only experienced cavers can visit this lake and other remote locations in the cave.

Rushing water roars through Lilburn Cave.

Inside Caves

It's dark in there! When Walter first explored the cave, he and his companions must have used oil-filled lanterns and candles to light their way. Now, visitors on a first-time tour of Crystal Cave can see the formations with the help of electricity. Recently a solar panel system to capture sun power has been added, replacing generators. They are also treated to pitch-black darkness at one point on their tour. By turning off the lights, the tour guide provides an experience of total lack of light inside a cave, even in daytime.

The temperatures inside Sequoia Park caves range from 62 degrees Fahrenheit to nearly freezing. The park's lowest elevation cave, Kaweah, at an elevation of 1,600 feet above sea level, maintains a cool 62 degrees Fahrenheit. Caves at higher elevations exist in a colder neighborhood. One of the highest is Alto Cave, located in the Mineral King area of the park. At 10,000 feet in the mountains, it is much colder at 33 degrees Fahrenheit - just above freezing. In fact, the temperature of a cave is usually equal to the average annual temperature of the outside air.

Formations found within a cave are not seen above ground. A stalactite forms when water dripping from the roof of a cave leaves minerals behind, and a tapered rock forms, pointing down. A stalagmite is similar to a stalactite, except that it starts on the floor of a cave and is made by drips from above.

Cave pearls can also be found in caves. They form in shallow pools or small pockets where water drips. Dripping water coats a grain of sand or small pebble. It also moves it, preventing it from adhering to the bottom of a pool.

Ancient People In The Caves

Joel Despain, Cave Specialist, tells about finding bones. "While working at Crystal Cave in the 1980s, I was shown several sites with bones. In 1992, I showed the sites to Harold Werner, Sequoia Park biologist. Werner took one look at a jawbone and pronounced, 'This is human.'"

Physical anthropologist Peter Howell examined the same remains the following year. He found six bone fragments from two individuals. One was an adult male who was more than thirty-five years old when he died. The other was from a child who would have been seven to nine years old.

The wear on the teeth in the jawbone shows that these bones are those of American Indians who died and were buried in the cave many years ago. The Inyana (known today as Yokuts) and other Native groups ate acorns, chia seeds, and other food ground in bedrock mortars. Small grains of hard stone that mixed with the grain left their teeth with a unique pattern of wear.

Also, in 1993, cave guides found a deposit of charcoal near the Crystal Cave entrance. It was determined that it came from a tree that died between the years 1600 and 1820. The charcoal was found where natural light has its farthest reach into the cave. It was the best place to start a fire to light torches for exploration.

Hector Franco, an American Indian, says, "When the people who acted as caretakers for these sites [the caves] died, their bodies or ashes were often buried at that site."

We can only imagine the lives of the two whose bones were found in the cave. Perhaps they represent many others who explored the caves hundreds, maybe thousands, of years ago.

FIG. 6.6 Photo credit © Dave Bunnell

Cave pearls form in shallow pools or small pockets where water drips. Dripping water coats a grain of sand or small pebble. It also moves it, preventing it from adhering to the bottom of a pool.

MARY MARTIN WEYAND

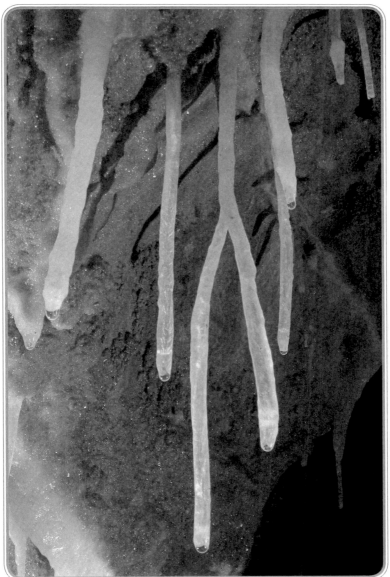

FIG 6.7 Photo credit © Dave Bunnell

Soda straws form when slow-seeping water enters through a cave's ceiling. If the straw becomes plugged, the water begins to flow on the outside surface. The soda straw may gradually transform into a stalactite.

Palmer Cave - An Ancient Place

On November 12, 1872, a hunter and trapper, Joseph Palmer, found a large cave that he named Palmer Cave, after himself. The entrance is an irregular opening in the roof of the cave, about 10 x 20 feet. Upon entering the cave, it becomes larger, like an upside-down funnel. To reach the cave floor, it's a 60-foot sheer drop from the entrance. Three large rooms form the cave, and all are in perfect condition, with beautiful stalactites and stalagmites and one outstanding pillar.

For years at a time, people lost track of where Palmer Cave was located, due to its small entrance and remote location. The entrance, hidden below cliffs of granite on a ridge, is located three thousand feet below a solitary road. Only the physically fit make the difficult climb from the road to the small cave opening. Some cavers say that it's worth the hard climb to see the charms of a place that is at least 788,000 years old. It might be the oldest cave in the park and is the highest-elevation cave found to date.

To enter, the cavers go through an opening in the cave ceiling, and they must rappel (controlled descent on a rope) down to the floor. There they find gypsum, a mineral that is generally white or clear. Its crystals can grow as clusters of see-through needles, as curling twisting "flowers" on walls, or as hanging clumps of " hair" composed of thousands of fine, long crystals. While small, Palmer Cave is lush and beautiful.

Soda straws form when slow-seeping water enters through a cave's ceiling. If the straw becomes plugged, the water begins to flow on the outside surface. The soda straw may gradually transform into a stalactite.

Clough Cave

❝ *Clough Cave was discovered by William Clough, a miner and prospector, on April 6, 1885. It was a beautiful cave for its stalactites, stalagmites, and pillars. But these have been broken and carried away by the hundreds. People heard of the cave and came to see, as it was easy to reach. Much of what remains has been blackened by pine torches used in exploration, all of which happened prior to the park being named in 1890. Because this cave is now protected, it is gradually and slowly restoring itself. Dripping water from the ceiling continues to deposit its load of dissolved minerals, building new crystals, stalactites and stalagmites."*

- Walter Fry, Nature Notes, January 20, 1925

Home To Unique Animals

Since 1925, more people have harmed the Clough Cave. In 1997, rangers arrested three men leaving the park with stolen cave items in their possession.

This is troubling because the cave is home to animals found nowhere else in the world. They have adapted to the dark and become new species.

The eyeless Calcina Cloughensis is only found in Clough Cave.

Like a spider, this arachnid (Calcina cloughensis) has eight legs. Unlike a spider, it has a single, nearly round body segment. It is a predator that hunts down and eats other cave life. This animal has certain physical features suited to its cave environment. It has extra-long antennae, the lack of coloration, and longer limbs for moving across rough, open surfaces. Because it lives in total darkness, it has no need for eyes.

Another animal found in Clough Cave is known to most people as the sow bug or pill bug. The fourteen-legged isopod in the cave is translucent and white with long antennae that constantly explore the ground ahead. It eats organic matter including roots, sticks, leaves, and bat guano.

These underground-dwelling animals have developed adaptations for cave living and are called Troglobites. There are at least seven, perhaps nine, species of unique animals in Clough Cave. People who broke or removed cave items in the past also damaged the animal's habitat.

Bats And People

Some animals use caves on a regular basis but do not complete their life cycles there. They are called Trogloxenes. Bats are a good example. Some kinds of bat like to roost in caves to sleep by day, leaving each evening to hunt for food. The little brown bat, (Myotis lucifugus), is believed to regularly use Crystal Cave as a daytime home.

(Troglophiles) use caves, but can just as easily not do so. In Sequoia Park, (troglophiles) include black bears, ringtail cats, and people. (Hey, that's us!) People, as well as these animals, use caves for purposes of hiding, sleeping, or exploring.

It's a good idea to take nothing but pictures and leave nothing but footprints when you visit a cave.

The "curtains" in Pumpkin Palace are inspected by cave explorer Vivian Loftin.

FIG 6.9 Photo credit © Dave Bunnell

Many scientists study caves.

- Speleologists study and explore caves, and nothing else.
- Anthropologists study the bones and tools of people who lived many years ago.
- Biologists study live people and animals - what they do and how they function.
- Geologists study the history of the earth by observing rocks and landforms.
- Hydrologists study the content, flow, and movement of water.

An Organization For Cavers

In 1941, the same year that Walter Fry passed away, the American cavers organized themselves into the National Speleological Society (NSS). Their purpose is to explore, conserve, and study caves in the United States.

Hurricane Crawl Cave - A New Find

Experienced cavers Joel Despain and Robert Childs found Hurricane Crawl Cave in 1986. Most of it was explored between 1986 and 1995, and it was mapped by 1999. Its name refers to the incredible flow of air blowing out its small entrance.

Wind whips through some caves.

- In Hurricane Crawl Cave, as well as in Crystal Cave, winds originate ... in what is known as a chimney effect. In "Hidden Beneath The Mountains", author Joel Despain explains, "On hot summer days in the mountains, warm air enters cracks, holes, and entrances leading into the upper levels of caves. There, the air cools and sinks downward, creating a current that increases as the day warms. The wind finds lower entrances and openings where it escapes back to the surface."

Junior Caver Tour In Crystal Cave

Are you between the ages of 8 and 13 Years? If so, and if you are in good physical condition, able to climb over large rocks and have no fear of small or enclosed spaces, you can go on this 1.5 hour tour. You will be provided the necessary gear and will take the tour with two trained cave naturalists. There is a fee, and these tours are conducted only during summer months, so check in with Sequoia National Park for more information.

In Summary

Sequoia 6. Crystal Cave - Then and Now

- ✓ Walter visited a few caves, but he believed there were more. He was right! Now, 265 caves have been discovered, with probably more to be found.
- ✓ Tiny animals have evolved in the darkened Sequoia caves, and many are found nowhere else on earth.
- ✓ Bats use the caves as places to sleep and nest.
- ✓ The caves, damaged by people, are now better protected than they were in Walter's day.
- ✓ Except for Crystal Cave, permits are needed to visit Sequoia and Kings Canyon caves. Some caves are not open to the public.
- ✓ Previously unknown caves are still being discovered.
- ✓ Through the National Speleological Society, experienced adults can lead youth groups safely through caves.

SEQUOIA 7

American dipper birds are found on and near fast moving streams.

SEQUOIA 7.
The Bird That Walks Underwater

Just as Walter Fry was awestruck by the American Dipper so many years ago, you can be equally amazed today. If you've tried standing up in rushing water, such as the Kaweah River in springtime, you already know how easy it is to lose your balance. You don't have webbed feet, and neither does the American Dipper. Yet it can dive into and walk along the bottom of a fast-moving stream with ease.

> ### The American Dipper - A Big Mistake
>
> ❝ *I was camped at Marble Fork River in Sequoia National Park . . . when I noted a pair of [dipper] birds (Cinclus mexicanus) darting back and forth through a thin sheet of water that poured over a fall in the river and formed a swirling pool in a white marble basin some ten feet below. By wading and crawling in under the [waterfall], I found a nest had just been started on a moss-covered rock (that stuck out like a shelf), about four feet back of and beneath the falling water, and I decided to watch the procedure . . . until it was completed.*
>
> *"I made a trip to the nest every third day and until the twenty-seventh day. I found the nest completed in every detail and it had one egg in it. Eggs were deposited every other day until*

there were five eggs laid. My trips to the nest greatly annoyed the birds that cried zit, zitzit scolding notes as they fluttered about my head.

"This is how the [dippers] built their nest: The birds began by digging a small excavation down through the moss to the rock; from this they rolled the moss out on all sides so as to form a compact ring ten inches across and one and one half inches thick. The uprooted moss in the ring was then woven and tied in with the growing moss . . . [thus forming a solid foundation]. Using a portion of this ring for a threshold, next a circular, upright arch ring for the door was built which gave a round opening four inches across. This ring was made up of . . . moss . . . and thoroughly anchored . . . the base to the foundation ring. To this structure, bits of moss were added day by day to build up the sidewalls and roof.

"By the twenty-first day the birds had completed the exterior shell and started to build the nest within. For the interior, only dead, yellow pine needles were used. As they chose only pine needles, it was interesting to note how the birds got them through the waterfall. They carried but one pine needle at a time and grasped it in their beak by the larger end, so this is extended backwards along side of and against the body when flying. The entire structure was completed in every detail.

"After all the eggs were deposited, I decided to remain away, but after a lapse of some five weeks . . . I decided to take just one more look. . . . I had crawled in under the [waterfall] and stood within about four feet of the nest when five baby [dippers] poked their fuzzy heads out of the door of their nest, blinked their eyes, and looked at me. They showed no evidence of fear. I admired them for a few minutes only, and had just turned to go away, when all of a sudden one of the

parent birds came dashing through the waterfall and buzzed frantically about my head, uttering shrill zit, zit, zit scolding notes of anger and fear. . . All five of the young birds scampered pell-mell from the nest, went head over heels down the wet slick rocks, where they were caught by the waterfall and dashed into the swirling pool below.

"At this I jumped out from under the [waterfall] and into the . . . swirling pool in an effort to save the birds from immediate drowning. . . . The fledglings [were carried by the current] close to the bottom of the pool. . . . All the while they were flapping their little pinfeathery wings and working their feet in a desperate attempt to rise to the surface.

"I rescued two of the birds and enclosed them in my hat. One of the parent birds, which was fluttering over my head, happened to see one of the young floating near, and dived in after it; and by swimming close in front of it, steered the fledgling downcurrent to shore, where it scrambled over the wet, slick rock to safety. Then a second bird was brought to safety by the same method.

"Apparently, the fifth bird had been drowned, for it had given up the struggle and was lying motionless in the bottom . . . about six feet under water; but when I dove down and brought it to the surface and held it by the feet, head downward, allowing the water to run out of it, it soon revived.

"I kept the young birds in my hat in order to let them warm . . . after which I carried them gently into the nest whence they came. A few minutes later, one of the parent birds hurried to the nest, rejoined the much disturbed offspring."

- Walter Fry, Nature Notes, August 14, 1929

Dippers build intricate nests, often under waterfalls or bridges.

Stunning Abilities

"They're absolutely amazing," commented one biologist. "I can't even stand up in these streams, but here are these tiny birds that dive right into raging white water."

With slate gray feathers, the American Dipper blends in with the rocks and water. At 7 and one half inches long, it is larger than a sparrow and smaller than a robin. It has a short tail, pale legs, and yellowish feet.

The dipper also communicates with a beautiful singing voice. It sings throughout the year and in all kinds of weather. John Muir, the man who named the Giant Forest (of Sequoia National Park), loved the dipper bird and described its song as one that is matched to the music made by the water. He said, "The dipper never sings in chorus with other birds nor with his kind, but only with the streams."

The American Dipper got its name because of its telltale dipping motion. It bends and straightens its knees as much as sixty dips per minute. Even young birds practice dipping while still in the nest. Adult birds do it when resting between feeding dives, and they dip faster when seeking a mate or when alarmed. Some naturalists wonder if this action, like everything else about dippers, is tied to the bird's rushing-water surroundings. Perhaps the up-and-down motion changes the light angle, allowing dippers to see into the water. Or, maybe it just helps these little birds keep fit for those incredible dives into raging water. It's also possible that they signal to one another by dipping when stream noise makes it hard to hear one another. That would be like using hand signals to catch someone's attention, or communicating through sign language.

A Nose Clip And An Extra Eyelid

Perfectly suited to its way of life, dippers have a flap of skin that covers the nostrils while in the water. You might say they have a built-in nose clip!

Another unusual fact is that the dipper often appears to be winking. This comes from a thin sheet of skin, something like an extra eyelid. It moves fast, giving a flashing effect, and seems to clear the eye of watery spray and splashes. This is separate from the action of the bird's eyelid, and is called a nictitating membrane.

A waterproof feathered coat protects the dipper.

Dippers preen to oil their feathers.

The Purpose Of Preening

Dippers' feathers are kept waterproofed by the abundant oil from a preen gland above the tail. Like a painter, dippers dab their bill in this gland, then spread the oil on their feathers, a "do-it-yourself" raincoat! Even in the coldest weather, a very thick undercoating of down feathers keeps the dipper warm.

A Habitat Of Swift Running Water

Even in heavy snowstorms, the dipper can be found year-round at the same mountain streams and waterfalls. Unlike other locations in California where waterways have been rerouted, dams built, or lakes created, the park's waterways remain the same as they were when Walter watched the dippers.

Yearly frequent storms and heavy snowfalls bring deep snow to higher elevations of the mountains. When spring arrives, the melting snow continually feeds the waterfalls. In Walter's time, the snowpack averaged fifteen to twenty feet deep. In the 1990s and during the first decade of the twenty-first century, it has averaged only half as much, arriving in the form of rain with a smaller amount of snow. When this happens, less year-round water is available for the dipper's habitat.

Flexible Home-Builders

In years when the snowfall is less, and the waterfall is small, what's a dipper to do? When an ideal nest location is not available, these industrious birds establish nests in other spots. Nests have been found among upturned roots of fallen trees, near or over the water. Some birds have used the underside of bridges, tucking a nest in between the girders that hold up a bridge.

It might be more perilous for the dipper to nest in these alternative places, as they can be accessible to the water snake, mink, marten, skunk, weasel, or other stream-frequenting animals that prey on dippers. During the nesting period and while the young remain dependent, the mother and nestlings give off no body odor. As most of the dipper predators depend on their sense of smell to find a meal, the mother and young are hard to detect.

An Unusual Kitchen

Most people go into the kitchen and peer into the refrigerator or open a cabinet door to look for a snack. Dippers find their food in an odd place: in, on, or under cold, swift-running water.

In six to ten feet of water, while holding its wings out slightly to steady itself, the amazing dipper not only stays upright but hunts for and catches water-living insects from the bottom of the streambed. Starting from a boulder in the stream, it dives into the tumbling stream. In less than a minute, it pops to the surface, a tasty insect larva in its bill. Returning to the boulder, it downs its juicy meal. In summer, the dipper might find food along the shallow edges of rivers or streams. It is seen wading along, ducking its head under water to turn over pebbles and fallen leaves with its bill. Soon the dipper finds a favorite, the larva (wingless and often wormlike feeding form) of the mosquito, the caddis fly, or the mayfly.

You might find larva in your own yard.

- The larva of an insect is a feeding form that hatches from an egg. For instance a caterpillar is the larva of the butterfly or moth.

- Water bugs, water beetles, and other forms of life are also snapped up by the dipper. When they catch small fish, they take it ashore where it's devoured. Water-landing insects, such as water striders, are also fair game for the industrious dipper. Swimming like a duck, the dipper uses its feet as paddles as it flaps along the surface to reach its prey.

- In cold weather, the dipper can be seen snatching frozen insects from the surface ice of lakes or from snowbanks. Even in snow or frozen water, the dipper seems to be in harmony with its surroundings.

Caring For Youngsters

While still in the egg, the chick develops a spot on its upper beak that sticks out. This spot is sharp and allows the chick to peck its way out of the shell. Within a few weeks of hatching, the spot or "egg tooth" disappears.

The newly hatched chicks cry for food often, and it takes the efforts of both parents to catch food. At the peak of the day, both mother and father hurry back to the nest twelve times an hour to feed their begging hatchlings.

Chicks are fed even after they leave the nest. One day, a mother dipper was spotted with a fat insect in her beak. She landed near a newly fledged bird and tried to place the insect in its bill. The youngster dropped it. The mother picked it up and flew to a branch that sloped into some water. She dipped the insect into the water and then flew back to the youngster. Again, the small bird dropped its food. The mother retrieved the insect and flew to the same branch, repeating the ritual, then returning to the baby. At last the insect was swallowed.

A parent to the rescue, as a nestling begs for food.

You might wonder about the amount of bird waste produced by such hungry eating machines. It's surprising to learn that the young birds, when defecating, turn their tail toward the nest entrance and, with a clearly visible expulsive effort, shoot fecal mass four to six inches out of the nest. These masses are eliminated in a thin covering, a membrane called a "fecal sac." We might think of it as something like a tiny plastic bag. Many of these sacks roll directly into the water and are carried downstream. No diapers to wash! Wouldn't it be nice if human babies had such a gift for parents?

Only eighteen days after pecking their way out of the eggshell, the newly feathered chicks follow one another out of the crowded nest. They jump directly into the water. The parents, flying at short distances, encourage the fledglings as they hop from one river rock to another. Soon, the young seem to know instinctively how to run, climb, dive and swim, or flutter along the surface of the water.

In Summary

Sequoia 7. The American Dipper - Then and Now

✓ The American Dipper can still be seen in the waterfalls and streams of Sequoia National Park.

✓ It is unknown if there are more birds, the same number, or fewer dipper birds in Sequoia and Kings Canyon National Parks than in Walter's day.

✓ The watery habitat that the dippers love is still abundant in Sequoia Park. The smaller snowpacks of more recent years might have put stress on the birds.

✓ The streams and waterfalls of the Sequoia and Kings Canyon National Parks have remained undisturbed.

✓ The insects that are food for the dipper birds are still available.

SEQUOIA 8

Wood chips fly as this pileated woodpecker chops his way into the trunk of a tree.

SEQUOIA 8.
Blazing Topknots

Long before you catch a glimpse of this large black and white woodpecker with its red crest, you will hear it. Seemingly louder than other birds, its calling and drumming sounds are used to deliver messages throughout the forest. The male calls are a lower pitch than the female. Shrill and loud calls are given when a bird encounters a rival or another pair in their territory.

The Pileated Woodpecker
A Family Tragedy

We [a troop of soldiers* and myself] were camped at the Parker Group of Big Trees in Sequoia National Park. Early in May 1911, a pair of (pileated) woodpeckers (Dryocopus pileatus) was observed foraging near the camp . . . At first, the birds appeared to be afraid of us. But in a few days, they became quite tame and allowed us to approach them.

"Near [our] camp kitchen, the birds chiseled out a chamber in the side of a large fir (tree) stump. The nest hole was twenty-four feet above ground, thus making it easy for our inspection [using] a lineman's climbing outfit. The opening was 7 and one half inches across, with a downward tunnel fourteen inches deep and expanding to ten inches in diameter [at the lowest part of the hole]. The bottom was covered with a fine layer of bits of wood. Four eggs were laid in the nest, one each on May 7, 8, 9, and 10.

Do You Know?

To climb a tall tree calls for safety equipment.

✪ A lineman's outfit is used to work on power lines. Shoes with spikes, a large sturdy belt to encircle the tree, and a hardhat are the main pieces of climbing gear.

❝ *We became greatly attached to the birds, and applied the names of "Cap" and "Phoebe" to the pair. Each bird took its turn in occupying the nest . . . while the other was off feeding; but at night, Phoebe always occupied the nest, while Cap roosted in the doorway with his head outward. After the eggs were hatched, both birds were in quest of food during the daytime for their young; but after nightfall, each bird took its regular station at the nest.*

"A happier pair of birds I never saw than these as they went forth each day in performance of their household duties. All went well with the family until the evening of June 16 when a sad disaster befell them and resulted in the death of Phoebe.

On this fatal day, as Phoebe was in flight near her nest, a savage Cooper's hawk (Accipiter cooperii) darted, struck, and killed her.

"Cap, having witnessed the killing of his mate, seemed terror stricken. . . . For two nights and a day, he sat sadly in the door of his nest, until we became alarmed lest the young birds would starve.

"But early on the morning of the 18th, he seemed to fully realize that he now had a double duty to perform in caring for his beloved offspring. By this time, the young birds were so hungry that they kept up a continual chirping in their begging for food. So, soon after daylight, Cap sallied forth into the forest and, like a dutiful father, gathered and carried food to his young with frantic effort. So successful were his labors that by noon the young birds became quiet, their appetites having been satisfied.

"While Cap was away on one of his trips, I climbed the stump in order to get a good look at the young birds by using a flashlight. . . . To my great satisfaction, I espied four fuzzy heads swaying about on long, slender necks, with their four mouths gaped wide open, ready to receive food.

"The fledglings were about one-fourth grown and covered over with a fluffy down of light grayish-brown, which blended to a somewhat darker color about the head and neck. It is difficult to realize that these homely little creatures develop into such handsome birds.

"Cap worked diligently day after day to gather food for his brood. During the nights, he covered them on the nest. As time went on, his labors became more and more strenuous, for the young were growing larger and required more food. Finally they became so large that they would climb into the nest door and await Cap's return with morsels for them.

"On the morning of July 19, the young could endure their housing no longer, and as Cap flew out from the nest they all sailed out after him. Not yet having become versed in the art of flying,

OF GIANTS AND GRIZZLIES

> they soon hit the ground with a thud. [Cap seemed to be] filled with fear and anxiety and tried to encourage them to return to the nest. Failing in this, he led out through the trees, collecting food from nearby stumps and logs, with his brood flapping and scrambling along after him.
>
> "For several days the birds remained about the camp, with the proud father always leading the procession; but they finally drifted away. For eight years thereafter, pileated woodpeckers nested at the Parker Group of Big Trees, and every time I see one of these beautiful birds I wonder if it is one of the lineal descendants of dear old Cap and Phoebe."
>
> - Walter Fry, Nature Notes, November 23, 1931
>
> *Army troops helped to protect the park.

A Colorful, Noisy Creature

Now, about one hundred years after Walter had his experiences with "Cap" and "Phoebe," pileated woodpeckers still thrive in Sequoia National Park. Males have a red forehead, crown, and crest, giving them a startling appearance. Females also have a red crest, though smaller, starting from the crown of the head.

MARY MARTIN WEYAND

Like this busy adult, Cap had four hungry mouths to feed.

Sometimes, the large nest entrance and big interior becomes home to other species.

Along with the flash of red on the top of the head, the bird appears to be mostly black and white. The underside of its wings has large white patches that can be seen when it flies overhead. A perched bird shows white on the side of the neck.

The noise of drilling can be heard over long distances. The large woodpecker clings to a tree while it strikes one hard blow after another. The frontal bones of its skull project out over the base of the upper-half of its beak, absorbing the impact.

In making its large nesting holes, the direct hit with its beak has been measured at 600 to 1,500 g-force. That's many times faster than a survivable car crash, which is measured at 100 g's. If people were to bang their heads that hard, they would be badly injured. The unique design of the woodpecker skull prevents injury to their brains.

FIG 8.4 Illustration silhouettes. orig. credit: © Mahesh Iyer and L Shyamal

About the size of a crow, the pileated woodpecker is the largest woodpecker in Sequoia.

FIG 8.5 Photo credit © Ryan Somma

The skull of a pileated woodpecker is built to withstand drilling for food and constructing nest cavities.

Not only do woodpeckers make a lot of noise while excavating, but their call of [cuk, cuk, cuk] resounds loudly through the trees. As if that isn't enough noise, they often drum their bills. Drumming is done by tapping their beaks against a tree without making a cavity hole. Scientists believe that drumming is used to announce their territory, or to communicate with a mate. One way they can be found is to follow their drumming and excavating sounds in the forest.

Do You Know?

Woody Woodpecker became a cartoon favorite.

- An animated cartoon character, Woody Woodpecker, was inspired by the pileated woodpecker. The cartoon character was originally created by Walter Lantz, who was born on April 27, 1899 in New York. Lantz was inspired to create the character when a pileated woodpecker constantly pecked on the roof of his honeymoon cottage.

Where Do They Live?

Pileated woodpeckers choose a thick forest that contains old, dead and decaying trees with broken branches and limbs called "snags." In the old-growth forest areas of the Giant Forest in Sequoia, these colorful, crested birds have been known to nest in Crescent Meadow and also in the area of the Parker Group of trees, 2 and one half miles from the Giant Forest Museum.

When people removed trees in old-growth forests, as they did when Walter worked for the Smith Comstock sawmill, pileated woodpeckers were robbed of their homes. Now the Sequoia and Kings Canyon National Parks are protected. This is one of the reasons people are not allowed to remove downed firewood from certain areas of Sequoia National Park.

Research says that 3,904 acres of old-growth forest would have from three to six pairs of pileated woodpeckers. How much room is that? A football field covers about one acre of ground. So 3,904 acres of old-growth forest would be the same as 3,904 football fields laid end-to-end. These woodpeckers need lots of space in the forest.

The Building Bird

Pileated woodpeckers make an unusually large hole for their nest. The entrance to the nest is made at a level of 15 to 125 feet above the ground. They drill out an oval-shaped entrance hole measuring approximately 4 inches wide and 6 inches tall. After drilling through the bark, they drill downward, excavating a cavity 12 to 30 inches deep into the tree. It is at the bottom of the cavity that the female lays her eggs on fine wood chips.

Building A Home For Others

The woodpeckers build a fresh nest cavity each year and rarely use a nest from previous years. You can notice that woodpeckers have been at work, building a new nest cavity, when you see fresh wood chips at the base of a tree.

Multiple exits allow escape routes from this roosting tree.

The old nest cavities are big enough for other larger cavity-using birds and mammals. Perching birds such as swallows, bluebirds, chickadees, wrens, or house sparrows raise their young in the abandoned woodpecker nests. Small-to medium-size mammals such as bats, squirrels, chipmunks, mice, and raccoons might move in. Even tree-climbing snakes and tree frogs have been found in former woodpecker homes. Because these animals make nest cavities used by other species, biologists say the pileated woodpecker is a "keystone species."

Do You Know?

Pileated Woodpeckers help other animals.

✣ A keystone species is one that benefits other species of animal. Because pileated woodpeckers create large cavities used by other animals, it is considered an important contributor to its ecosystem.

Nest Robbers And Predators

Not only do woodpeckers make large nest cavities to raise their family, they also make holes, called roost chambers, in other trees so they can escape from predators, such as the Cooper's Hawk.

The roost chambers are much larger than their nests and have more than one entrance. The birds use these chambers for safety and for rest at night.

Today's parent birds must be fierce protectors of their young, as well as of themselves. Several kinds of hawks and owls, as well as the American marten and the gray fox, hunt birds in the forest, and nestlings can be snatched. Bears and raccoons sometimes succeed in tearing into the cavities when the wood is too rotten or the walls are thin.

Chipmunks, squirrels, deer mice, and weasels are known to raid nests. A number of birds, including jays, crows, and other species of woodpeckers, prey on eggs and nestlings.

A watchful eye is kept for hawks and owls, fox and martens.

What's For Dinner?

Carpenter ants are the pileated woodpecker's number-one meal. These ants nest in moist wood, including rotting trees, tree roots, tree stumps, and logs or boards lying on, or buried in, the ground. To obtain such tasty food, the bird removes bark from trees and digs a hole so it can reach the long, narrow passages made by the ants. Then it uses its long tongue to catch and extract ants. In fact, a biologist found that one pileated woodpecker had 2,600 ants in its stomach contents.

The larva of the wood-boring beetle is the second-most important food, along with other insects, berries, and fruits, when available.

Other insect-eating birds are often attracted when pileated woodpeckers uncover ant nests. They swoop down and enjoy the feast. This is another contribution to other species by the keystone pileated woodpeckers.

Do You Know?

Do people eat ants?

✪ Ants and other insects are a good source of protein. Do people really eat ants? Some do. You can buy chocolate-covered ants. Some people think that honeypot ants, (Myrmecocystus), are the tastiest.

Pileated woodpeckers, like many birds, have learned to solve problems when searching for food. For instance, when probing a tree with their beaks, sometimes the food they take out of the tree is dropped. The woodpeckers have been seen catching dropped food by quickly hunching forward while extending a wing a little on the side where the item is falling. At the same time, it presses its chest against the tree trunk. If the save is successful, the food will be caught in the pocket formed by the wing and the chest against the tree trunk. Then, with its beak, it recovers the food.

Raising Their Brood

When a nesting tree is chosen, both the male and female pileated woodpeckers work on the cavity. Sometimes, after they've partially dug out a home, they decide to leave it and go to another spot and start over. We can only guess that there is something about their first choice that no longer works for them. Sometimes, in the next year, they actually do use the nest site that they'd left unfinished the previous year.

Once eggs are laid, one or the other parent stays on the nest. Unlike other birds, the male almost always roosts on the eggs overnight, but not always. You might recall that "Phoebe" was the one who covered the eggs each night.

Do You Know?

Some bird-related definitions.

❂ A hatchling is a bird just out of the eggshell.

❂ A nestling is a young bird after it's hatched until it leaves the nest.

❂ A fledgling is a feathered youngster that has left the nest.

❂ Regurgitation is the casting-up of food from the bird's crop. This would be somewhat like "storing" a piece of food in the cheek of your mouth, then using your tongue to move it to the center of your mouth and spitting it out.

Nestlings are constantly hungry, and their rapid growth is due to a protein-rich diet. Parent birds collect ants and ant larvae in their crop (a pouch in the throat area) to carry food to their nestlings. Upon reaching the nest, they regurgitate the contents into the open mouths of their young, providing a portion for each nestling upon each visit.

When it is time for the young birds to leave the nest, the parents encourage them by making fewer feeding visits. The parents invite their young to fly by calling and drumming near the nest tree. It was unusual that "Cap's" youngsters followed him without a summons. The youngsters' first flight is a weak effort, much like a human baby taking its first walking steps. Within one to several days, the fledglings are capable of flying well.

Most bird species quickly part from their parents once they've left the nest. Instead, pileated woodpecker chicks stay with their parents for several months. They receive meals and learn how to find ants in the ground, as well as in the trees. Because ants are found only underground during winter months, the young birds must learn how to find them by watching their parents.

In Summary

Sequoia 8. The Pileated Woodpecker - Then and Now

- ✓ The number of pileated woodpeckers may have decreased when trees were cut down. The numbers have probably improved since tree-cutting stopped in Sequoia National Park in 1890.
- ✓ Though lumbering removed mature trees, old-growth forest remains and provides possible nesting sites.
- ✓ Biologists call pileated woodpeckers a "keystone species" because other forest animals can use their abandoned nest cavities.
- ✓ As a keystone species, they also uncover food sources, especially in winter, that provide food for themselves and other species.

SEQUOIA 9

The Steller's jay is a noisy, raucous fellow and beautiful when you get a glimpse.

SEQUOIA 9.
A Circle Of Life

Often nature presents a "balancing act" that surprises us. For instance, in the early 1900s a surprising amount of blue jays were noticed as Walter and other park personnel worried about the many dying pine trees in Sequoia National Park. It was not unusual to see the jays among pine trees gathering seed, but there were many more than usual.

> ### A Serious Attack
> ### A Solution, Other Than Fire
>
> ❝ *In 1918 pine beetles* were killing the yellow pine and sugar pine trees. So sudden and serious was the attack of these beetles that we worried that all the pine trees would be destroyed.*
>
> *"We were quick to realize the threatened danger, and it was decided that all affected trees would be cut and burned, thus destroying the larvae of the young beetles while they were in the wood. While we were busy with this project, we noticed that a vast number of blue jays (Cyanocitta stelleri) had congregated and many had nested in the infested area.*

> 66 One day a sharp-shinned hawk (Accipiter striatus) swooped down and killed a female blue jay. Men came running and scared away the hawk before it could carry off the dead bird. We examined the blue jay, and to our great surprise we found in its mouth and throat were eight western pine beetles and fourteen mountain pine beetles.
>
> " . . . As we looked at the dead bird, we wondered; and as we wondered, we thought of their destiny and of the many hundreds or perhaps thousands of years these birds have been helping to save the forests we have with us today.
>
> - Walter Fry, Nature Notes, December 2, 1931
>
> *western pine beetle (Dendroctonus brevicomis) and mountain pine beetle (Dendroctonus ponderosae)

One Change Causes Another

The gathering of the blue jays was in response to a change that happened in their environment. With the arrival of so many beetles, the birds responded by quickly gathering to eat their fill of beetles, a part of their regular diet. These birds had probably been saving the pine trees from beetle infestations for many hundreds, or even thousands, of years. Most likely the men realized that in the future they could put aside their ideas about burning trees to eliminate the beetle threat.

A New Branch Of Science

In 1866, when Walter was only seven years old, the new word "ecology," the study of organisms and their environment, was first created. But it wasn't until he was an older man that it became popular as a branch of science. An ecology system, or ecosystem, is made up of a community of plants, animals, and other living organisms, together with the environment, including soil, air, water, and sunlight. Throughout his life, Walter studied how the elements of the Sequoia and Kings Canyon National Parks' ecosystem worked together, resulting in a balanced system of continuing forest life.

YOU Have An Ecosystem

- Your ecosystem includes your family and your neighborhood, the air you breathe, and the water and food you consume. It includes the insects and the domestic and wild animals in your neighborhood, as well as the plants that grow in your yard, and in your neighbors' yards.

- The size of an ecosystem can be large, such as the entire Sierra Nevada range of mountains. The Sierra Nevada includes Sequoia and Kings Canyon National Parks, and (for example) Huckleberry Meadow, Crystal Cave, and the Kaweah River ecosystems. Unlike the precise edge of a basketball court, each system's boundary blends with others.

- Because they are side-by-side, Sequoia and Kings Canyon National Parks can be considered as one ecological unit. An ecosystem can be as large as these two combined national parks, or as small as a single tree. It can even be much smaller - a puddle of water or even a scientist's test tube filled with microscopic creatures.

A Constantly Adjusting Ecosystem

In Walter's time and still today, wind blowing from the Pacific Ocean sweeps up grains of sand and dirt from California's Central Valley and carries it to the mountains. Deposited in the park, these particles sink into the ground where earthworms and the tiniest of creatures live and die. The remaining carcasses, along with spent flowers, decayed leaves, and animal droppings, continually improve the soil. Plant roots, including the giant trees, take their nourishment from the enriched ground. Many interactions occur within an ecosystem every moment of every day. The following description gives us some idea of how an ecosystem functions.

With their large ears, mule deer constantly listen for enemies.

Between towering redwoods, a fawn rises from its hidden resting bed and follows its mother to a stream for water. It dislodges bits of soil and tree leaves when it bends for a drink. The rushing water carries the dirt and leaves over a waterfall. Some of the leaves get caught in a half-built American dipper bird nest. The birds nudge the leaves into the side of the unfinished nest and go about their busy task of nest-building. The remaining loosened soil dances to the bottom of the streambed and settles among the pebbles, providing nutrition to the small insects that hover at the bottom. Soon, a dipper bird dives to catch an insect for lunch. Having ingested tiny creatures from the stream, the bird returns to a tree, and bird droppings fall to the ground, adding minerals to the soil. The soil feeds the trees and shrubs that grow along the streambed, and the young deer nips off tender buds for a morning meal.

Like the mule deer (Odocoileus hemionus), people who come into the park become part of the ecosystem. From leaving a pine cone where it is found, to carrying out food wrappers, people's actions can make a direct difference to the ecosystem.

A Good Idea?

Even before Walter's time, people thought it would be a good idea to add rainbow trout (Oncorhynchus mykiss) to the forest lakes. Some brought buckets of live trout and added them so they would multiply. This way, the people reasoned, they could catch and eat the trout every year. What they didn't know is that trout are very aggressive feeders. The trout ate the other fish and the frogs that were once abundant in those lakes. The mountain yellow-legged frog (Rana muscosa and Rana sierrae) has almost disappeared.

FIG 9.3 Photo credit © Adam Backlin/ USGS

The mountain yellow-legged frog is eaten by trout.

The arrival of rainbow trout, at a place where they had not naturally been, caused a huge change in the ecosystem of the lakes. For instance, with fewer frogs, disease-carrying mosquitoes might increase in numbers, biting both humans and animals alike.

In recent times, an effort has been made to correct this error. Park scientists used nets to remove the nonnative fish from eight of the lakes in Sequoia. In all cases, frog and tadpole numbers increased rapidly following fish removal. Since then, the California Department of Fish and Game and the National Park Service have removed more nonnative fish. Now, as some lakes become free of the trout, the mountain yellow-legged frogs are more numerous. Each spring, there are more and more tadpoles in these lakes.

Bee's are pretty tasty!

Almost crow-sized, Clark's Nutcracker will beg for food at campsites.

OF GIANTS AND GRIZZLIES

FIG 9.6 Photo credit © Dave Powell, USDA Forest Service

Whitebark Pine Trees can become diseased.

As he traveled throughout the park, Walter would often pause to watch the animals and birds of the park. No doubt, he watched a crow-sized bird, the Clark's nutcracker (Nucifraga columbiana), collect pinecone seeds from one of the whitebark pine trees (Pinus albicaulis) that dotted higher elevations of the forest. When its chin pouch was stuffed, it would fly away to hide the seed for retrieval during the winter.

Today the bird's favorite tree, the whitebark pine, is fewer in number. The tree's orangish color, a result of blister rust, a tree disease, is noticeable on the hillside even in summer when leaves are generally green. The disease came to the United States on seedlings imported from Europe beginning in 1907. This disease infected the trees in the eastern United States. The disease traveled across the United States and was first noticed in Sequoia in 1941. The valued whitebark pine tree was used by many birds and by bears that gorged on its seeds. Due to disease, there are fewer of these trees, and the animals must find other food sources.

Both of these changes, the addition of trout to lakes and the introduction of blister rust, were caused by people's actions. You would not say that people were doing something wrong on purpose. But what they did had unforeseen consequences.

The Mountain Air

Other changes can be noticed. When you arrive in the parks, one of the first things you might like to do is to take a hike up a mountain trail and reach a lookout. This is a spot where you can see distant mountaintops and peer down canyons so deep that a river or a stream at the bottom looks like a tiny rivulet. At this viewing vista in summer, you might notice a band of brown haze near the horizon. Instead of seeing clearly, you gaze through a layer of pollutants, commonly called smog.

Riding The Wind

As you look at the mountainous landscape, you wonder how the brown layer of pollution got into the park. The pollutants mostly come from the actions of people. Outside the park, at private homes, bug spray might be used to chase away the insects that invade a family's vegetable patch. Instead of a safe "green-friendly" product, we can imagine for a moment that a more toxic insecticide is used. While some of the spray lands on the plants, the breeze coming from the ocean picks up the remainder of the sprayed particles on its way up a canyon. These particles hitch a breezy ride on the wind into Sequoia Park. It is a small amount and might be unnoticed since it's from just one sprayer.

You can see a brown layer of pollutants in Sequoia and Kings Canyon National Parks on some days.

But what if many households use polluting sprays? What if an entire orchard is sprayed with toxic chemicals? What if a factory makes a mistake when they burn their waste and expel polluting chemicals into the air? Add to this mix the nitrogen dioxide that comes out of the exhaust pipes of cars and trucks burning gasoline all day long. Combined, all of these pollutants from many sources produce poor air quality for the park.

FIG 9.8 Photo credit © Robert L Anderson, USDA Forest Service

Bad ozone levels caused these Jeffrey pine needles to be mottled (yellowed and unhealthy)

When The Air Is Polluted

Ozone, a form of oxygen, can be good or bad, depending on where it is. Ozone is good when it is high up in the atmosphere and shields people, animals, and plants from the sun's harmful ultraviolet rays. "Bad" ozone forms near the ground when sunlight starts reactions among the different polluting chemicals.

You can see the effect of "bad" ozone by noticing Jeffrey pine trees (Pinus jeffreyi). These ozone-sensitive trees show extensive injury to their foliage from park ozone levels. For example, one study found that nearly 90 percent of Jeffrey pines in or near the Giant Forest in Sequoia show signs of damage. "Bad" ozone damages chlorophyll in the needles, reducing or destroying their ability to photosynthesize (make food for the plant).

The Water Everything Drinks

A long hike may bring you to one of the 3,200 lakes or ponds, or to a spot along the 2,600 miles of rivers and streams in Sequoia and Kings Canyon National Parks. Appearing pure, the water might actually contain the same polluting particles that damage air quality.

During the dry summer and fall, small airborne particles (the same ones that make the air a brown color), land on the water and collect on the ground, rocks, and trees. These polluted particles are washed into the water by thunderstorms, winter rain, snowfall, and snowmelt. Air pollution is the biggest cause of park water pollution.

Solutions to improve air quality are at the top of the issues for the two parks.

A Big Enough Drink?

Can you imagine being thirsty but getting only one teaspoonful of water? The amount of available water depends on the annual amount of rain and snowfall each year. This is measured by how much snow has piled up in the mountains. When Walter was in the park, the annual snowpack was close to twenty feet each year.

In the last thirty to forty years, the air temperature has become warmer. Some scientists say that this is caused by human use of chemicals. Other scientists say that this is a natural cycle of the planet earth. Some believe it is a matter of being a bit of both. Regardless of the cause, we can see that a warmer climate brings about changes for the parks' plants and animals.

From 1970 until current times, the snowpack has been much less, closer to ten feet each year. Our now warmer climate translates into less rainfall and snowfall, and the ecosystems involved have less water to use. Wise water usage, both in Sequoia and Kings Canyon National Parks as well as in the entire state of California, is a primary concern.

People Make A Positive Difference

Today, many people are making a positive difference to the Sequoia and Kings Canyon ecosystems. For instance, the home of the big trees, Giant Forest, has been restored. The removal of over three hundred buildings was followed by an effort to help the Giant Forest recover the scarred land to a more natural state. Three different solutions were tried; (1) replacing the soil to allow seeds to develop on their own, (2) performing controlled burn of the undergrowth, and (3) planting seedlings of the native plants where the buildings had been. The best results came from number 2, the controlled burn of the Giant Forest area. This method produced the fastest recovery in the Giant Forest.

OF GIANTS AND GRIZZLIES

> ### Nature's Ever-Changing Circle
>
> *In his 1932 summary of a Twenty-Five Year Survey of Animals of Sequoia National Park [1906 to 1931], Walter said,*
>
> *"It is indeed fortunate that we have the National Parks. They illustrate the benefits of . . . conservation and the natural balance of wild life . . ."*
>
> *- Walter Fry, Nature Notes, 1932*

John Muir, the famous naturalist, said in his book, "My First Summer in the Sierra", "When we try to pick out anything by itself, we find it hitched to everything else in the universe."

As people learn to become better caretakers, the circle of life will continue to bring richness to those who follow Walter Fry's footsteps across the Sequoia and Kings Canyon National Parks.

In Summary

Sequoia 9. A Circle of Life - Then and Now

- ✓ Ecology, the study of organisms and their environment, was introduced when Walter was a boy.
- ✓ Within an ecosystem, changes brought by one element influence all the other elements.
- ✓ Blue jays gathered to eat a sudden influx of pine beetles, showing a balance of nature.
- ✓ The addition of rainbow trout disrupted the natural balance of frogs and mosquitoes.
- ✓ Recovery of the lakes to their native state is in progress.
- ✓ Blister-rust-diseased seedlings were brought into the United States, and they spread to the Sequoia in 1941. Scientists seek a way to control blister rust disease.
- ✓ Chemicals degrade air and water quality in the park. Efforts to improve air quality are a number one concern.
- ✓ Giant Forest has been cleared of buildings, protecting the future for the landscape and the wildlife.

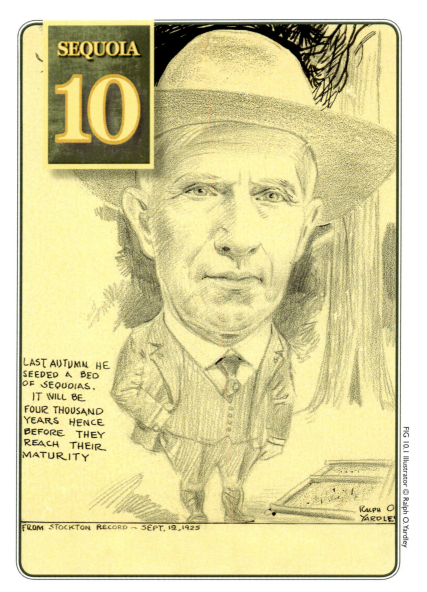

Walter Fry was well-known in the Central Valley.

SEQUOIA 10.
Walter Fry, A Curious Naturalist

Even before he was grown, young Walter Fry dreamed of going west. Then it happened. In 1869, Walter's family left his birthplace, Watseka, Illinois, to move to Fredonia, Kansas. During the six-hundred-mile trip, ten-year-old Walter rode next to his father on the hard board seat of their covered wagon. After traveling for over a month, they arrived at their destination in Kansas on a late summer morning. He got his first glimpse of the small prairie town that would be their new home.

The land was as flat as a dinner plate, and when he scrambled from the wagon, he couldn't see over the top of the thick, tall prairie grass. Walter was disappointed, as the tales he had heard and stories he had read had led him to believe that traveling westward would bring him to tall mountains and vast rivers.

FIG 10.2 Photo credit © Weldon Schloneger

Walter was hoping for mountains and tall trees!

OF GIANTS AND GRIZZLIES

He no doubt treasured articles about California from publications like "Scribners Monthly" magazine. Walter probably read "A visit to the Great Yosemite," (now Yosemite National Park) published in August, 1871. The article, written by a person known only as S.J., took a group of adventurous adults from the eastern United States to see California for themselves. The author detailed how they hired a man and a boy as guides. In Mariposa, California, where their trip into the vast mountain range and the giant trees began, they acquired the services of the fifteen-year-old. The youngster was one of the keenest speculators in firearms and horse trading that S.J. had ever met. "I shall never look upon his like again." Surely, Walter would have liked the boy right off.

The Yosemite article further described the size of one giant sequoia. "One mighty tree that had fallen by fire and been burned out, into which we walked for a long distance, we found to be inhabited; a grizzly had made his nest there. The tree was forty feet in diameter . . . and must have been four hundred feet high.' The author went on to say, "I have not met a single person [on the east coast of the United States] who believes the literal truth which travelers tell about these marvelous giants."

Walter wanted to see not only the trees, but also the four-thousand-feet high granite rock described in the article. "'Tu-toch-ah-nu-lah's cliff', or in english 'El Capitan'" kept his dreams of going west fired up.

When he was not attending school, he worked the Kansas family farm with his father. Although he was a good student, he favored learning all there was to know about farming and raising cattle. By the time he finished school in 1877, he was an accomplished horseman and trusted cattleman.

By age 28, Walter Fry was married to Sarah Ann Higgins and owned a ranch and a herd of fine cattle. They had three children, but sadly, in 1887 his two younger children died during a fever epidemic (diphtheria and typhoid fever took many lives in Kansas in the 1880s). In the same year, all of his cattle became diseased and died.

140

Walter Fry, age 16. His first formal portrait, 1875, photographer unknown

His money gone and his days sad, Walter longed to see the richness of the California mountains that he learned about as a child. He obtained a map of California and found the location of Tulare Lake, and the tall mountains.

He and Sarah sold their Kansas ranch and left for California with their surviving son, Clarence. They stepped off the train in the railroad town of Tulare, California, on March 24, 1887, and were immediately awestruck by the beauty of the snowcapped Sierra Nevada (mountains). Walter had finally arrived at the place he'd dreamed about for so long.

In September of that same year, they welcomed a baby girl named Bessie. With a need to earn money to support his family, Walter tried his hand at various jobs, including railroading, ranching, and farming. During their first years in California, the family

OF GIANTS AND GRIZZLIES

lived in the Central Valley, near Terra Bella, California, and also in the city of Tulare. In those days of horse-drawn carriages and 'putt-putting' automobiles, the mountains still seemed a distance away. Walter remained on the lookout for a way to live and work closer to the mountains.

The Slaying Of A Giant

Sometime after arriving in California, Walter noticed an advertisement for "tree fallers," men hired to cut down trees, posted by the Smith Comstock Sawmill Company. Needing better pay, he applied. He took a job as an axman and reported to the Big Stump Basin where the sawmill operated [in an area that became Sequoia National Park].

On that first day of work, the sun brought heat. Walter wiped away the sweat that gathered under his hat, leaned back as far as he could, and peered upward at the gigantic tree. Its beauty touched him, and he felt sad that it would be cut to the ground. Like thousands of other trees, its top thrust into the bright blue sky and seemed to touch the fluffy clouds. The underside of massive limbs cast shade on him and the four other workmen.

The foreman decided which way the tree would fall, and he marked the location of the cut. Using wood from other trees, the axman's first job was to build a platform to stand on because the place for cutting was located above the bulging tree base. Swinging as hard as he could, Walter and another axman began to chop into the giant tree, their striking strokes sending wood chips flying. After delivering one blow after another for hours, it was finally the end of the workday. Walter rubbed his sore arm muscles as he headed home on his horse.

The next day at sunup, he resumed delivering heavy blows. After several days of chopping, a large V-shaped undercut reached the heart of the tree. Walter set down his ax, and other men took over. It was the job of the two-man saw team to pull the double saw back-and-forth from the opposite side of the large cut that had been axed away. A series of steel wedges were then pounded into the sawn cut until the tree began to fall. When warned that the majestic tree was about to fall, Walter ran a safe distance away. He held his ears as the giant tree swayed and crashed to the ground. The sound was tremendous, louder than a freight train, and it rang in his ears. The ground shook as if an earthquake had hit. A cloud of dirt and leaves flew into the air and covered him. Walter sneezed and coughed away the dirt from his throat as he climbed over boulders and branches to inspect the fallen sequoia tree.

FIG 10.4 Photo credit © NPS SEKI Archives

A downed giant sequoia. A man holds two two-men saws bound together. The saw was pulled back-and-forth to cut through the tree after the ax-men had done their part. The names of those pictured are unknown.

Walter felt small next to the downed tree. The shorn bottom of the tree was on its side. The stump was much wider than he was tall. He felt small standing next to the cut that towered over his head. How long had this giant tree stood its watch in this ancient forest? He touched the severed wood, breathing in the rich smell. Walter peered closely at the rings that circled from the outer edge to the very center. He guessed that the center circle was the first tiny ring formed in the first year of the tree's life.

That evening, as Sarah pinned together the material for a new dress for little Bessie, Walter thought of the tree. He borrowed a box of pins and slipped them into his pocket.

The next day, Walter returned to the downed giant sequoia. He lay across the stump and pinpointed the middle. He knew each ring represented a year. How many years had this tree lived? Starting with the center, he counted . . .

One, two, three, four, five, six, seven . . . He used a magnifying glass because the divisions were difficult to see with the naked eye. He stuck one of Sarah's pins in each successive ring and zigzagged them across the section. He reached one hundred years. Leaving a pin to show the one-hundredth ring, he pulled out ninety-nine pins and used them to count the next one-hundred rings. He did this again and again. Leaning back, he looked at the rings and saw that he had counted only a small amount, with many more to go. Walter continued counting to five hundred years. Still there were many more rings. He finally reached one thousand, and then two thousand. As huge sadness coursed through him, he kept counting, passing three thousand years.

At last, he reached the growth ring for the current year - the last outer ring of the tree: 3,266 years!

He stood and stared at the huge stump, then shook his head. Cutting down these ancient giants seemed like a horrible thing to do.

Walter threw down his ax and quit the job.

At the time, he thought that Big Stump Basin was the only place where the sequoias grew. Later, upon learning that there were other groves, Walter vowed to save the remaining giant sequoia trees.

He was one of the first to sign a petition in the fall of 1889 to establish Sequoia National Park, in hopes of a new law that would protect the trees from any further abuse of the ax and the saw. President Benjamin Harrison established the park one year later, and in 1895, Walter moved his family to Three Rivers, the gateway to the new Sequoia National Park.

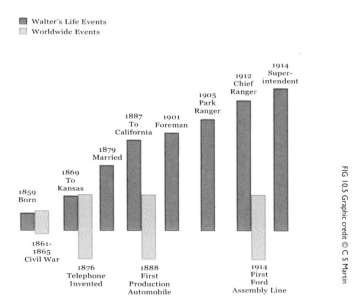

FIG 10.5 Graphic credit © C S Martin

Many Jobs In Sequoia National Park

Beginning July 5, 1901, Walter was hired as the Sequoia Road Construction Foreman. After being a construction foreman, he was hired as a park ranger, chief ranger, superintendent, and finally as the park commissioner.

When he was the commissioner, Walter co-wrote Big Trees, with John R. White, then superintendent of Sequoia National Park. The book was published in 1930 by Stanford University Press of Stanford, California, and shows Walter's deep understanding of the Giant Sequoia trees.

Eventually, he was known as "the Grand Old Man of the Sequoias," as he spent so many years in the park. For many of those same years he was the final legal authority in the park. He settled disputes, conducted marriages, and performed many legal duties. People called him "Judge Fry," though he was not actually a judge. He retired in 1930, yet continued to serve Sequoia National Park until his death in 1941.

Walter astride his horse, "Maude," with his spaniel "Mark" in 1904 while riding in Giant Forest. Walter traveled more than 50,000 miles on the back of a horse through Sequoia and (what later became) Kings Canyon National Park. That's equal to twice around the world.

Walter's Well-known Friends -
Hale Tharp And The Potwisha Native Americans

In Sequoia National Park today you can inspect the house hollowed out of a fallen giant sequoia. Tharp created the unusual mountain home by carving the home-inside-a-log in 1858, and he stayed in his odd dwelling each summer while his cattle grazed on mountain grass. Tharp told Walter, "I first located my ranch near the Kaweah [River] in the summer of 1856. The Indian Chief, 'Chappo,' was a fine man. I was the first white man that had ever come to their country. The Indians all liked me because I was good to them."

Walter visited, as he did often, with Hale Tharp.

66 *This is the account as I obtained it from him (Hale Tharp) on May 25, 1910: When I (Tharp) first came to the Three Rivers country in 1856, there were over 2,000 Indians [Potwisha, a subgroup of the Monache or Western Mono Native American Tribe] living along the Kaweah River above Lemon Cove. Their headquarters camp was at Hospital Rock. That was the seat of government where all tribal business was transacted and festivities were held. Chief Chappo, his council, and the medicine men lived there. The camp was never vacated during either winter or summer, and the campfires were kept burning continually. All the Indians who were sick, extremely old or crippled, as well as most of the women with young babies remained there the year round. During the summer months a great many of the Indians went to the higher mountains, but the camp at Hospital Rock was always kept filled."*

- Walter Fry, Nature Notes, February 17, 1925

Evidence of Native American habitation has been traced back five hundred to six hundred years, to approximately AD 1300-1400. Today, when you visit Hospital Rock located along Generals Highway, you will see evidence of native pictographs. Along the river, you will see grinding stones made of rock, along with many similar-looking round holes where native people ground acorns, pine nuts, and other seeds into meal (like flour). They easily caught fish from the Kaweah River, located near the rock.

Near Hospital Rock, you can climb Moro Rock.

Native Americans writing, hundreds of years ago.

No one today can interpret the writing.

Lying under Hospital Rock, you can see outside.

John Muir, A Famous Explorer

In the summer of 1901, to Walter's great surprise, the famous conservationist John Muir arrived and introduced himself. Walter was thrilled to meet the person who, in 1875, had given the area of big trees the name "Giant Forest." Their visit was repeated in 1902, when Walter again enjoyed visiting with Muir.

Walter spoke about the famous man when interviewed in 1938. "John Muir was one of the world's greatest explorers, a man who usually went alone, leading a pack mule or horse, or often on foot with only a hunting sack and a smack of food, sometimes penetrating the hills without blankets or thought of shelter."

By then 63 years old, Muir had a long, flowing gray beard, yet he was quite fit for a man his age. Walter remembered reading that Muir had started his career by walking from Indiana to the Gulf of Mexico in 1868, a distance of one thousand miles.

Walter enjoyed his visit with Muir, a gifted writer of ten books and three hundred articles about the wonder of Sequoia, Yosemite, and other parks. In the same year that Walter Fry met him, Muir published the book, Our National Parks, and he is called the "Father of our National Park System."

Walter especially enjoyed sharing the park with children, and here we see him inspecting a pinecone with his grandson, Russel Weckert.

FIG 10.11 Photo credit © Fry Family Archives

Today, in case of disaster

Years ago Walter helped people learn that the trees should be protected. Now, young people are doing a better job. Young people are hired by the University of California, and Cornell University to climb the great trees and collect some of the seed cones. Why are they doing this? In case of a catastrophe in the forest, we would have seed set aside to replant these largest of trees. These young men, unlike mountain climbers, ice climbers or rock climbers, are the only ones who climb living organisms. It is dangerous work and Walter Fry would, for sure, be proud of this effort.

In Summary

***Sequoia 10. Walter Fry, A Curious Naturalist -
Then and Now***

- ✓ In 1869, ten-year-old Walter rode a covered wagon to Kansas. When grown, he owned a cattle ranch.
- ✓ Walter left Kansas after the loss of two children. With his remaining family he arrived in California in 1887.
- ✓ Walter took a job as an axman and cut down a giant sequoia. He quit when he counted its 3,266 tree rings.
- ✓ In 1889 Walter was one of the first to sign a petition to create Sequoia and protect the big trees.
- ✓ Walter worked at Sequoia National Park as a road foreman, a park ranger, the first park superintendent, and park commissioner.
- ✓ In 1930 Walter wrote Big Trees, with then superintendent John R. White.
- ✓ John Muir, the famous naturalist and Walter Fry visited together on several occasions.
- ✓ Walter left behind journals and nature notes, with stories shared throughout Of Giants and Grizzlies.

IN ENDING

"Fry's real love lay not in administration but in the forests and among the wildlife of his park home. Over his years in the parks, he had become obsessed with nature study, an obsession that would soon pay rich dividends for the visitors."

- *Challenge of the Big Trees, 1990,*
Sequoia Natural History Association, Inc,
Larry M. Dilsaver and William C. Tweed.

LEARN MORE

By-chapter Video and Audio clips are available to you by following the link listed below.

You will find by-chapter selected videos, shared with Of Giants and Grizzlies by wonderful nature enthusiasts.

Enjoy!!!

www.writeonforkids.com/LearnMore.pdf

Love the book? We'd love to hear your own nature tales! Write to us at mweyand@sbcglobal.net

Mary Martin Weyand
Write On For Kids

GLOSSARY

Sequoia 1.
1. germinate: (jur mi nat) to cause to sprout or develop...pg. 13
2. petrified: (pe tre fi ed) to turn into stone. Minerals left behind by water petrify wood by replacing wood cells when they die ...pg. 5
3. phenomenon: (fe no me non) a rare or significant fact or event ...pg. 3
4. spectral: (spek tral) of or relating to a spector; ghostly ...pg. 3
5. vascular: (vask ye lar) a channel for the conveyance of fluid (example; vein carries blood) ...pg. 11

Sequoia 2.
1. ecosystem: (e ko sis tem) a community of living things interacting with their environment, especially under natural conditions ...pg. 30
2. headwaters: (hed waw terz) the streams that form the beginning of a river ...pg. 23
3. muzzle: (mu zel) the open end of a weapon from which an object is expelled ...pg. 21
4. thicket: (thi kit) a thick, usually small, patch of shrubbery ...pg. 20

Sequoia 3.
1. espied: (i spi d) to catch sight of ...pg. 34
2. malodorous: (ma lo de res) having a bad smell ...pg. 34
3. onslaught: (on slawt) a violent attack ...pg. 36
4. repast: (ri past) the act of taking food ...pg. 34
5. scavenged: (ska vinj) to collect usable things from what has been discarded ...pg. 40
6. wafted: (woft ed) to move lightly by ...pg. 34

Sequoia 4.
1. carnivorous: (kar ni ve res) feeding on animal tissues …pg. 52
2. entangled: (in tang geld) to become twisted together in a mass hard to straighten out …pg. 51
3. environmentally: (in vi ern ment al lee) the whole complex of factors (soil, climate, living things) that influence ability to survive…pg. 62
4. larvae: (lar ve) a young wingless, often wormlike form …pg. 62
5. pupae: (pu pe) a stage of an insect between larva and adult, usually in a cocoon …pg. 62
6. tentacle: (ten te kel) long, flexible structure that sticks out from an animal (like an octopus), usually around head or mouth …pg. 51

Sequoia 5.
1. talus: (ta les) a pile of rocks found at the base of a cliff or steep slope …pg. 68
2. carnivores: (kahr nuh vores) an animal that eats flesh …pg. 74
3. musky: (muhs ke) the smell of a strong body odor …pg. 74

Sequoia 6.
1. antennae: (an te na) a pair of slender, movable organs of sensation of the head of an arthropod (like a crab) - Antennae are used to feel and smell. …pg. 90
2. pillar: (pi ler) a column, an upright support …pg. 88
3. rappel: (ra pel) to descend by sliding down a rope …pg. 88
4. stalactite: (sta lek tight) a deposit of calcium carbonate resembling an icicle hanging from a roof …pg. 85
5. stalagmite: (sta lag might) a deposit of calcium carbonate from ceiling drips, formed on a cave floor …pg. 85

Sequoia 7.
1. frantically: (fran tik a lee) marked by fast and nervous activity …pg. 97
2. pell-mell: (pel-mel) in confused haste …pg. 97
3. scampered: (skam pered) a playful, hurried movement …pg. 97
4. threshold: (thresh hold) entrance; usually the wood or stone beneath the door …pg. 96

Sequoia 8.
1. espied: (i spi d) to catch sight of ...pg. 109
2. excavating: (ek ska vit ing) to hollow out ...pg. 113
3. foraging: (fo rij ing) to graze; search for food ...pg. 107
4. regurgitate: (ri gur ji tat) throw back undigested food; out again ...pg. 119

Sequoia 9.
1. chlorophyll: (klo ra fil) the green matter in the leaves and stems of plants that is necessary to produce food for plants from sunlight. on plants; for photosynthesis ...pg. 134
2. infestation: (in fes ta -shen) to spread or swarm in or over in a troublesome manner ...pg. 124
3. insecticide: (in sek ta sid) a chemical used to kill insects ...pg. 132
4. nitrogen dioxide: (ni tra jen di ok sid) an air pollutant formed from automobile exhaust ...pg. 133
5. photosynthesize: (fo to sin the siz) The process in green plants and certain other organisms by which carbohydrates are synthesized from carbon dioxide and water using light as an energy source. Most forms of photosynthesis release oxygen as a byproduct. ...pg. 134

Sequoia 10.
1. epidemic: (e pa de mik) an outbreak of disease ...pg. 140
2. habitation: (ha bi ta shen) being in a dwelling place; in a community ...pg. 148
3. smack: (smack) a small quantity of food ...pg. 149

RESOURCES

Sequoia 1.

Fry, Walter and White, John R., Big Trees, Stanford, CA., Stanford University Press, 1930.

Fry, Walter, The Discovery of Sequoia National Park and the Sequoia Groves of Big Trees, Nature Notes/Journal and Park Bulletins, National Park Service,13, June 12, 1923.

Grescoe, Audrey, Giants, Boulder, CO., Roberts Rinehart Publishers, 1997.

Hartsveldt, Richard J., Harvey, H. Thomas, Shellhammer, Howard S., Stecker, Ronald E. 1975,

A Brief History: National Park Service, San Jose University, California, http://www.nps.gov/history/history/online_books/science/hartesveldt/index.htm

Harvey, H. Thomas, Stecker, Ronald E., 1980, Giant Sequoia Ecology, National Park Service and San Jose State University, http://www.nps.gov/history/history/online_books/science/12.htm

Hill, Mary, Geology of the Sierra Nevada: Revised Edition, Berkeley, CA., University of California Press, 2006.

Johnston, Hank, They Felled the Redwoods, Costa Mesa, CA., Trans-Anglo Books, 1966.

Parsons, David J., Objects or Ecosystems? Giant Sequoia Management in National Parks, National Park Service, Three Rivers, California, 1992.

Parsons, David J., Nichols, H. Thomas, May 24-25, 1985, Management of Giant Sequoia in the National Parks of the Sierra Nevada, California, National Park Service.

Rumford, James, Sequoyah, Houghton Mifflin Publishing, Boston, MA., 2004.

Stecker, Ronald E., 4/6/2009, Arthropods Associated with the Giant Sequoia, National Park Service, http://www.nps.gov/history/history/online_books/science/12/chap6.htm

Tweed, William C., and Dilsaver, Larry M., Challenge of the Big Trees, Three Rivers, CA.,Sequoia Natural History Association, 1990.

Willard, Dwight, A Guide to the Sequoia Groves of California, Yosemite, CA., Yosemite Association, 2000.

Sequoia 2.

Brewer, William H. Up And Down California in 1860-1864: The Journal of William H. Brewer; 4th Edition, with Maps, University of California Press, Berkeley, California, 2003.

Fry, Walter, The California Grizzly, Nature Notes/Journal and Park Bulletins, November 4, 1924.

Storer, Tracy I., Tevis, Jr., Lloyd P., California Grizzly, University of California Press, Berkeley, California, 1955.

Grinnell, Joseph, PhD, California Grizzly Bears, Sierra Club Bulletin, 1938, pgs 70-81.

Gunther, Kerry A., June, 1995, Grizzly Bears & Cutthroat Trout, National Park Service http://www.nps.gov/yell/naturescience/beartrout.htm

Hittel, T. H., The Adventures of James Capen Adams:Mountaineer and Grizzly Bear Hunter of California, Kessinger Publishing Company, 2007.

Lee, Sonja, Research analyst, Bear Aware, Montana Magazine, November/December, Cover Story, 2007.

Peacock, Doug, Naturalist/Author, Yellowstone's Grizzly Bears Face Threats on Two Fronts, Environment 360 Magazine, Yale School of Forestry & Environmental Studies, Opinion, May 14, 2009.

Sequoia 3.

Bear Management Overview, National Park Service, Sequoia and Kings Canyon National Park http://www.nps.gov/seki/naturescience/ns_bears.htm

Breen, C., Paper; Biogeography of Gulo gulo (wolverine), San Francisco State University, http://bss.sfsu.edu/geog/bholzman/courses/FallooProjects/wolverine.html Department of Geography, Fall 2000.

Cabrera, Kim A., July 30, 2009, Black Bears, http://www.bear-tracker.com/bear.html

Copeland, Jeffrey P., USFS Retired, 2008; update 2012, Central Idaho Wolverine and Winter Recreation Research Study, The Wolverine Foundation, Inc., http://www.wolverinefoundation.org

OF GIANTS AND GRIZZLIES

Fry, Walter, A Wolverine vs. Two Bears, Nature Notes/Journal and Park Bulletins, National Park Service, Bulletin 19, June, 19, 1924.

Graber, David M., Paper; Winter Behavior of Black Bears in the Sierra Nevada, California, International Association of Bear Management and Research, 1990.

Jameson, E.W., and Peeters, Hans J., California Mammals, Berkeley, CA., University of California Press: revised edition, 2004.

Kilham, Benjamin, Among the Bears, New York, Henry Holt and Company LLC, 2002.

Masterson, Linda, Living with Bears, Masonville, CO., 2006, PixyJack Press.

Rogers, Lynn, Ph.D., Bear Facts; Live Camera Wildlife Research Institute, http://www.bearstudy.org, Ely, Minnesota.

Sleeper, Barbara, Wolverine: The Super Weasel, Pacific Discovery Magazine, Spring 1995, Pages 46-47.

United States Department of Fish and Game, 1998, Black Bear Management Plan-1998, http://www.dfg.ca.gov/wildlife/hunting/bear/docs/BlackBearMgmtPlan.pdf

Sequoia 4.

Baird, Carol J., Ph.D, Habitats Alive! Teacher Resource Guide, California Institute for Biodiversity, Oakland, CA., 2008.

Brown de Colstoun, Eric, March 29, 2010, How Does Your Garden Grow? National Aeronautics and Space Administration, http://soil.gsfc.nasa.gov/index.php?section=123

Cimons, Marlene, May 2, 2010, Why Human Blood Drives Mosquitoes Wild, Live Science, http://www.livescience.com/animals/mosquitoes-human-blood-bts-100122.html

Fry, Walter, The Sundew, Nature Notes/Journal and Park Bulletins, National Park Service, June, 1929.

Graber, David M., Status of Terrestrial Vertebrates, Sierra Nevada Ecosystem Project, Davis,University of California, 1996.

Holland, Jennifer S., Gold Dusters, National Geographic Magazine, March, 2011.

Ingles, Dr. Lloyd Glenn, March 27, 2010, Mountain Pocket Gopher,

Bureau of Land Management, http://www.blm.gov/ca/forms/ wildlife/

Kattelmann, Richard and Embury, Michael, Sierra Nevada Ecosystem Project: Final Report of Congress, Vol. III, Assessments and scientific basis for management options. Davis, University of California, Centers for Water and Wildland Resources, 1996.

Matthews, Kathleen R., Knapp, Roland A., Pope, Karen L., Garter Snake Distributions in High-Elevation Aquatic Ecosystems, Journal of Herpetology, Vol 36, No.1, 2002

Munz, Philip A., Introduction to California Mountain Wildflowers, University of California Press, Berkeley and Los Angeles, CA., 2003.

Pacific Tree Frog, March 26, 2010, http://www.blm.gov/id/st/en/environmental_education/BLM-Idaho_nature/wildlife/amphibians/ frogs_and_toads/pacific_treefrog_.html

Pidwirny, Michael, March 29, 2010, Soils, The Encyclopedia of Earth, http://www.eoearth.org/article/soil

Plants Profile; Drosera rotundifolia, Sundew; Dodecatheon jeffreyi, Sierra Shooting Star; Veratrum californicum, Corn Lily; Vaccinium uliginosum, Western Blueberry; United States Department of Agriculture, plants.usda.gov (http://plants.usda.gov)

Powell, Hugh, Web Team Editor, Yellow-rumped Warbler Life History, Cornell lab of Ornithology, http://www.allaboutbirds.org/guide/ Yellow-rumped_Warbler/lifehistory

Rosenthal, Sue, June 11, 2008, Buzz Pollination, BayNature Institute, http://baynature.org

Storer, Tracy I., Usinger, Robert L., Lukas, David, Sierra Nevada Natural History, University of California Press, Berkeley and Los Angeles, CA., 2004.

The Dragonfly Life Cycle, March 26, 2010, Dragonfly Site, http://www. dragonfly-site.com/dragonfly-life-cycle.html

Sequoia 5.

Bryner, Jeanna, March 20, 2008, Fossil of Oldest Rabbit Relative Found, Live Science, http://www.livescience.com/2381-fossil-oldest-rabbit-relative.html

Crist, Larry, Katzenberger, Diane, February 5, 2010, Endangered Species Act Protection for the American Pika Is Not Warranted, U. S. Fish and Wildlife Service, Press Release, http://www.fws.gov

Fry, Walter, The Hay Makers of the High Sierras, Nature Notes/Journal and Park Bulletins, National Park Service, Bulletin No. 8, August 24, 1922

Donald K., Journal of Biogeography, A brief history of Great Basin Pikas, Department of Anthropology, University of Washington, Blackwell Publishing Ltd. 2005.

Jeffress, Mackenzie, October 2009 and February 2012, Pika Research and monitoring at Craters of the Moon, University of Idaho, http://www.nps.gov/search/index.htm?query=pika+in+paril

McFarling, Usha Lee, A Tiny 'Early Warning' of Global Warming's Effect, Los Angeles Times, Los Angeles, CA., February 26, 2003.

Ray, Chris, Pikas and Climate Change: 2006 Report, University of Colorado, Ecology and Evolutionary Biology, Boulder, Colorado, http://www.colorado.edu

Santos, Nick; Gee, Marion; Griffis, Matthew and Clayburgh, Joan, Sierra Climate Change Toolkit: 3rd Edition, Sierra Nevada Alliance, 2010.

Storer, Tracy I., Usinger, Robert L., Lukas, David, Sierra Nevada Natural History, University of California Press, 2004.

Wallace, Linda, October 8, 2009, Memorable Moment with a Pika of the Sierra Nevada, http://www.pikaworks.com/pikas/latimes-article-303.html

Sequoia 6.

Barton, Hazel A., Introduction To Cave Microbiology: A Review For The Non-Specialist, Journal of Cave and Karst Studies, Kentucky, August, 2006.

Bradley, James V., Bats, Infobase Publishing, New York, NY, 2006.

Despain, Joel, Hidden Beneath The Mountains, Cave Books, Dayton, Ohio, 2003.

Fry, Walter, Caves of Sequoia National Park and their Discovery, Nature Notes/Journal and Park Bulletins, National Park Service,

January 20, 1925.

Hill, Mary, Geology of the Sierra Nevada, revised edition, University of California Press, Berkeley, CA., 2006.

NieKamp, Andy, Cave Exploring By Youth Groups, National Speleological Society, August 31, 2009, http://www.dugcaves.com/more/youth_article.htm

Rainey, William and Pierson, Elizabeth, 2002-2006, Bat Inventory of Sequoia National Park, http://science.nature.nps.gov/im/units/sien

University of Wisconsin at Eau Claire, 10/1/09, Biospeleology, University of Wisconsin, http://www.uwec.edu/jolhm/Cave/biospe2.htm

Sequoia 7.

Bent, Arthur Cleveland, Life Histories of North American Nuthatches, Wrens, Thrashers and Their Allies, June, Dover Publications, Inc., New York, 1964.

Burress, Rex, Those Funny Birds, Mount Diablo Audobon Society, September 25, 2009, http://www.diabloaudubon.com/birds/Rex/funny.html

Farrand, John, Jr. (Editor), Master Guide to Birding, Gulls to Dippers, Alfred A. Knopf, New York, 1983.

Fry, Walter, The Water Ouzel, Nature Notes/Journal and Park Bulletins, National Park Service, April 14, 1929.

Muir, John, The Mountains of California, The Century Company/The De Vinne Press, New York, 1894.

Reitsma, Bob, American Dipper: Daring to be Different, Smithsonian National Zoological Park, 2008, http://nationalzoo.si.edu/ConservationAndScience/MigratoryBirds/Featured_Birds/

Turbak, Gary, The Bird That Flies Through Water, National Wildlife Magazine, Jun/Jul 2000, vol.38, No. 4.

Sequoia 8.

Adams, Cecil, October 8, 1999, Do people really eat chocolate-covered ants? http://www.straightdope.com/columns/read/1351/do-people-really-eat-chocolate-covered-ants

Backhouse, Frances, Woodpeckers of North America, Firefly Books,

Ltd., New York, 2005.

Bull, Evelyn L., and Jerome A. Jackson, The Birds of North America, Pileated Woodpecker. Issue No. 148, Revised September 27, 2011 http://bna.birds.cornell.edu/bna/

Duncan, Sally, Coming Home To Roost: The Pileated Woodpecker as Ecosystem Engineer, Science Findings, issue 57, October, 2003, U.S. Department of Agriculture.

Fry, Walter, Pileated Woodpecker: Cock-of-the- Woods, Nature Notes/Journal and Park Bulletins, National Park Service, Bulletin No. 30, December 23, 1931

Hahn, Jeffrey, Cannon, Colleen, Ascerno,Mark, Carpenter Ants, 2008, University of Minnesota, http://www.extension.umn.edu/distribution/housingandclothing/DK1015.html

Hartwig, Carol L., Eastman, Donald S., Harestad, Alton S., Forest Age and Relative Abundance of Pileated Woodpeckers on Southeastern Vancouver Island, USDA Forest Service Gen. Tech. Rep PSW-GTR-181, 2002.

Monchka, Barret, May 18, 2009, Pileated Woodpecker Central, http://www.pileatedwoodpeckercentral.com/information.htm

Roberson, Don, June 21, 1997, The CREAGRUS California Counties Project: Tulare County, http://creagrus.home.montereybay.com/CA-TUL.html

Robinson, John C., California Partners in Flight Coniferous Bird Conservation Plan for the Pileated Woodpecker, USDA Forest Service, November 22, 2000, http://www.prbo.org/calpif/html-docs/species/conifer/piwoacct.html

Stonehouse, Bernard, Bertram, Ester, The Truth About Animal Builders, Tangerine Press, New York, June, 2003.

The Walter Lantz Cartune encyclopedia: Cartune Profiles: Woody Woodpacker, December 3, 2009, http://www.lantz.goldenagecartoons.com/profiles/woody

Timossi, Irene C., Woodard, Ellen L., Barrett, Reginald, H., Habitat Suitability Models For Use With ARC/INFO: Pileated Woodpecker, California Department of Fish and Game, Sacramento, CA., June 1995.

Sequoia 9.

Air Pollution Comes From Many Sources, June 27, 2010, http://environment.nationalgeographic.com/environment/global-warming/pollution-overview

Anteczak, John, Scientists find evidence of nearly extinct frog, July 29, 2009, California, A5, Los Angeles Times.

Barna, David, Flanagan, Colleen, Airborne Contaminants Study Released Measurable Levels Detected in Twenty Western U.S. And Alaska National Parks, February 26, 2008 National Park Service, U.S. Department of the Interior, News Release.

Bortz, Fred, Dr., Good Ozone; Bad Ozone, June 23, 2010, Ask Dr. Fred, http://www.fredbortz.com/askozone.htm

Brown, Matthew, Study: Pesticides prevalent in western national parks, Arizona Daily Star, February 27, 2008, http://www.azstarnet.com/sn/printDS/227147

Clark's Nutcracker and Pine Forest, Wild Birds Unlimited, Inc. June 10, 2010, http://www.wbu.com/chipperwoods/photos/clarks.htm

Cox, Sam, White Pine Blister Rust, January 2, 2003, http://www.landscapeimagery.com/wphistory.html

Ecosystem, New World Encyclopedia, April 3, 2008, http://www.newworldencyclopedia.org/entry/Ecosystem

Forest Economics, Sierra Forest Legacy, April 5, 2010, http://www.sierraforestlegacy.org/FC_FireForestEcology/FFFE_ForestEconomics.php

Fry, Walter, The Blue-Fronted Jay, Nature Notes/Journal and Park Bulletins, National Park Service, Bulletin No. 27, December 2, 1931.

Fry, Walter, A Twenty-Five Year Study of the Bird Life in Sequoia National Park-1906-1931, Nature Notes/Journal and Park Bulletins, National Park Service, Bulletin No.5, March 26, 1932.

Graber, David M., Facing a New Ecosystem Management Paradigm for National Parks, Ecological Restoration, Vol. 21, No.4, 2003, University of Wisconsin System and National Park Service. December, 2003.

Knapp, Roland, Dr., Introduced Fish, The Mountain Yellow-Legged Frog Site, February 2012, http://www.mylfrog.info/threats/introducefish.html

Polakovic, Gary, Polluted paradise, Los Angeles Times, September 13, 2005, http://www.latimes.com/travel/outdorrs/la-os-smog-parknew13sep13,1,3020800.story

Schoettle, Anna W., White Pine Blister Rust, USDA Forest Service, CO., November 14, 2008, http://www.fs.fed.us/rm/highelevation-whitepines/Management/Strategy/blister-rust-management

Storer, Tracy I., Usinger, Robert L., Lukas, David, Sierra Nevada Natural History, University of California Press, Berkeley and Los Angeles, CA., 2004.

The History of the California Environmental Protection Agency, January 19, 2006, http://www.calepa.ca.gov/About/History01/dpr.htm

Water Resources Overview, April 23, 2012, http://www.nps.gov/seki/naturescience/water.htm

Williams, Jack, Ozone can be both good and bad, depending on where it is, April 15, 2004, USA Today, http://www.usatoday.com/weather/resources/climate/2004-04-15-good-bad-ozone_x.htm

Sequoia 10.

Clemens, Earle R., John Muir Honored with Centenary Program at Sequoia National Park, The Terra Bella News, July 15, 1938.

Doctor, Joe, Collection of Judge Fry's Writings Real Treasure, Exeter Sun, August 1, 1978.

Elliott, John, Walter Fry: The Historian, Sequoia Sentinel, January 5, 1994.

Fry, Walter, Nature News Notes, Original (Compiled) Material provided by Walter Fry descendants, Joan (Perry) Thomsen and Rachel (Perry) Caggiano.

Judge Walter Fry Of Sequoia Is 82 Years Old Today, The Terra Bella News, March 14, 1941.

Judge Walter Fry Taken By Death At Woodlake; Funeral Rites Tomorrow, The Terra Bella News, November 19, 1941.

Rockwell, Mabel Macferran, Old Frontiersman Won Over Wilds, Widow's Ire (Hale Tharp), The Fresno Bee, October 3, 1954.

S.,J., A visit to the great Yosemite, Scribner's Monthly, Scribner &

Son, New York, August, 1871.

Sequoia Historical Society, The Life and Times Of Jessie Bequette (Video), 1991, Sequoia Natural History Association, Three Rivers, California.

Tweed, William C., and Dilsaver, Larry M., Challenge of the Big Trees, Three Rivers, CA., Sequoia Natural History Association, 1990.

MEDIA SOURCES

FIG 1.0 Photograph-Sequoia and Kings Canyon National Parks Map by U.S. National Park Service (2012 version of map, NPS) [Public domain], via Wikimedia Commons

FIG 1.1 Photograph-Giant Sequoia Hug; Family Hugging Sequoia Tree by Juan Camilo Bernal, 2012 Used under license from Shutterstock.com

FIG 1.2 Sequoia Tree Fossil, by Mary Martin Weyand, ©2013 All rights reserved.

FIG 1.3 Sequoia Tree Canopy, by Perri Martin, Provided by permission ©2013. All rights reserved.

FIG 1.4 Graph of Historical Timeline, by C S Martin, ©2013 Provided by permission. All rights reserved.

FIG 1.5 Photograph-General Sherman Tree by Perri Martin, Provided by permission ©2013. All rights reserved.

FIG 1.6 Photograph-Big Tree Seeds; Cone and Seeds by Mary Martin Weyand, ©2013 Provided by permission. All rights reserved.

FIG 1.7 Photograph-Longhorn Beetle Phymatodes nitidus, derived from 1975 drawing by Loren Green, ©2013 Provided by the NPS with permission. All rights reserved.

FIG 1.8 Photograph-Douglas Squirrel by Daniel Smith, 2012 Creative Commons licensed by PublicDomainImages.com

FIG 1.9 Photograph-Controlled Fire Burn by Rennett Stowe, 2012 Creative Commons licensed by Flickr.com.

FIG 1.10 Photograph-General Sherman with Fire Scar by Perri Martin, Provided by permission ©2013. All rights reserved.

FIG 1.11 Photograph-General Grant Snag Top Tree by Perri Martin, Provided by permission ©2013. All rights reserved.

FIG 1.12 Photograph-SEKI 1929 Tractor Forward, representation by NPS, ©2013 Provided by permission. All rights reserved.

FIG 2.1 Photograph-Snorkeling Bear; Coastal Alaskan Brown Bear by Lorraine Logan, 2012 Used under license from Shutterstock.com

FIG 2.2 Photograph-Standing Bear by Erik Mandre, 2012 Used under license from Shutterstock.com

FIG 2.3 Graphic-News Clip, by C S Martin, © 2013 All rights reserved.

FIG 2.4 Photograph-Brown Bear Crossing Log; Brown Bear in captivity by Numeristes, 2012 Used under license from Shutterstock.com.

FIG 2.5 Illustration-Claw comparison, representation by C S Martin

FIG 2.6 Photograph-Nursing Bear; Mother brown bear nursing four cubs by Jim Chagares, 2012 Used under license from Shutterstock.com.

FIG 2.7 Photograph-Mama Tells Cub; Brown Bears by Palko72, 2012 Used under license from Shutterstock.com.

FIG 2.8 Illustration-California State Flag courtesy Devin Cook, Creative Commons licensed by Wikimedia.

FIG 3.1 Photograph-Black Bear Makes a Face by Perri Martin, ©2011 All rights reserved.

OF GIANTS AND GRIZZLIES

FIG 3.2 Photograph-Bear Climbs Tree by Michelle Buntin, 2012 under Creative Commons license from Public-Domain-Images.com

FIG 3.3 Wolverine Resting On Rock, by Mats Lindh, 2012 under Creative Commons license.

FIG 3.4 Photograph-Black Bear Crossing the Road by Perri Martin, ©2011 All rights reserved.

FIG 3.5 Photograph-NPS Archive Dumpbears, representation by NPS, ©2011 Provided by permission. All rights reserved.

FIG 3.6 Photograph-NPS Archive Vehicle Damage, representation by NPS, ©2011 Provided by permission. All rights reserved.

FIG 3.7 Photograph-NPS Affixing Eartag, representation by NPS, ©2011 Provided by permission. All rights reserved.

FIG 3.8 Photograph-NPS Bear Paw to Human Comparison and Green Ink, representation by NPS, ©2011 Provided by permission. All rights reserved.

FIG 3.9 Photograph-Claw Marked Tree, by Kim Cabrera, ©2011 All rights reserved.

FIG 3.10 Photograph-Black Bear Scat, by Kim Cabrera, ©2011 All rights reserved.

FIG 3.11 Photograph-Bear Tracks, by Kim Cabrera, ©2011 All rights reserved.

FIG 3.12 Photograph-Newborn Black Bear Cubs by Mark Bertram, FWS, ©2011 Provided with permission. All rights reserved.

FIG 4.1 Photograph-Sundew (Drosera rotundifolia), by Scaners3D, ©2011 Used under license from Shutterstock.com.

FIG 4.2 Photograph-Wild Huckleberries, by Candace Hartley, Used under license from Shutterstock.com.

FIG 4.3 Photograph-Yellow-rumped Warbler, by Martha Marks, Used under license from Shutterstock.com.

FIG 4.4 Photograph-Corn lily Veratrum californicum closeup, by Dcrjsr gallery of Sierra flowers, August 15, 2010, by Wikimedia Commons.

FIG 4.5 Photograph-Dodecatheon jeffreyi, Sierra Shooting Star by Walter Siegmund, June 19, 2007, by Wikimedia Commons.

FIG 4.6 Photograph-Photo of a bumble bee close up, by Andrey Armyagov, Used under license from Shutterstock.com.

FIG 4.7 Photograph- Mountain pocket gopher, by Arleen Webster, January 17, ©2012, blogspot.com, with permission. All rights reserved.

FIG 4.8 Photograph-Sierran Garter Snake, by Joseph Uyeda - Pseudacris, ©July 5, 2008, Lassen County, CA., Provided January 27, 2012, All rights reserved, Used under license from Flickr.com.

FIG 4.9 Photograph-Pacific Chorus Frog, by Brendan Thornton, November 1, 2008, Retrieved April 4, 2012, Used under license from Dreamstime.com

FIG 4.10 Illustration-Mosquito/life cycle, by Jens Stolt, Used under license from Shutterstock.com

FIG 4.11 Photograph-Green Eyes, dragonfly by John A. Anderson, Used under license from Shutterstock.com.

OF GIANTS AND GRIZZLIES

FIG 5.1 Photograph-Pika On Rock With Berry, by Mark Byzewski, ©2012, All rights reserved, Used under license from Flickr.com.

FIG 5.1a Photograph-Mt. Whitney wilderness by Ben Kucinski, 2012 Creative Commons licensed by Flickr.com.

FIG 5.2 Illustration-Pika with shoe and shoelace by Carol Heyer, © All rights reserved.

FIG 5.3 Photograph-Pouncing Pika Carrying Grasses, by Carly Lesser and Art Drauglis, ©2010, All rights reserved, Used under license from Flickr.com.

FIG 5.4 Photograph-Short-tailed Weasel, by Ainars Aunins, Used under license from Shutterstock.com.

FIG 5.5 Photograph-Red-tailed Hawk, by Ron Rowan, Used under license from Shutterstock.com.

FIG 5.6 Photograph-Pika Sitting, by Mark Byzewski, ©2012, All rights reserved, Used under license from Flickr.com.

FIG 6.1 Photograph-A Junior Caver, by Dave Bunnell, ©2012, All rights reserved.

FIG 6.2 Outside Crystal Cave Entrance by Perri Martin, ©2008, All rights reserved.

FIG 6.3 Photograph-Crystal Sequoia, by Dave Bunnell, ©2012, All rights reserved.

FIG 6.4 Photograph-Crystal Cave Gate, Caden and Quinn, by Perri Martin, ©2008, All rights reserved.

FIG 6.5 Photograph-Inside a Sequoia Cave, Marble Walls, by Dave Bunnell, ©2012, All rights reserved.

FIG 6.6 Photograph-Cave Pearls Ursa Minor, by Dave Bunnell, ©2012, All rights reserved.

FIG 6.7 Photograph-Soda Straws Lilburn, by Dave Bunnell, ©2012, All rights reserved.

FIG 6.8 Photograph-Calcina cloughensis, by Dr. Jean K. Krejca, Zara Environmental LLC, ©2012, All rights reserved.

FIG 6.9 Photograph-Pumpkin Palace - Hurricane Crawl Caves, by Dave Bunnell, ©2012, All rights reserved.

FIG 7.1 Photograph-American dipper in rushing water, by Steve Byland, ©2010, Yellowstone National Park, Used under license from Dreamstime.com.

FIG 7.2 Photograph-American dipper at nest, Yellowstone National Park, by Don Getty, ©2012, Reprinted with permission, All rights reserved.

FIG 7.3 Photograph-Dippers feathered coat, by Sandy Sorkin, ©2012, Picasaweb, Reprinted with permission. All rights reserved.

FIG 7.4 Photograph-Dipper Preening, by Sandy Sorkin, ©2012, Picasaweb, Reprinted with permission. All rights reserved.

FIG 7.5 Photograph-Parent brings food, by Jim Zipp, Yellowstone National Park, ©2012, All rights reserved.

FIG 8.1 Photograph-Pileated Woodpecker Eating Insects, by Willie Lynn, ©2012, Used under license from Shutterstock.com. All rights reserved.

FIG 8.2 Photograph-Adult pileated woodpecker Dryocopus pileatus feeding, by Wayne Lynch, All Canada Photos, ©2012, All rights reserved.

OF GIANTS AND GRIZZLIES

FIG 8.3 Photograph-Male Pileated Woodpecker near hole, by Gregory Synstelien, ©2012, Used under license from Shutterstock.com. All rights reserved.

FIG 8.4 Illustration woodpecker and crow silhouettes, originals art by Mahesh Iyer and L. Shyamal, ©2012 under Creative Commons license.

FIG 8.5 Photograph-Pileated Woodpecker Skull, by Ryan Somma, ©2012 Creative Commons licensed by Flickr.com.

FIG 8.6 Photograph-Woodpecker Roosting Tree, by Mary Martin Weyand, ©2012, All Rights Reserved.

FIG 8.7 Photograph-Pileated Woodpecker outside my window, by Seabamirum, ©2012 Creative Commons licensed by Flickr.com.

FIG 9.1 Photograph-Steller's Jay in Dead Tree, by Steve Bower, ©2012, Used under license from Shutterstock.com. All rights reserved.

FIG 9.2 Photograph-Mule deer among giant trees, by Tim Briggs , ©2012 Creative Commons licensed by Flickr.com.

FIG 9.3 Photograph-Mountain Yellow-Legged Frog, U.S. Geological Survey Dept of the Interior/ USGS Photo by Adam Backlin, ©2012, with permission. All rights reserved.

FIG 9.4 Photograph-Clark's Nutcracker Eating Bee, by ND Johnston, ©2012 Used under license from Shutterstock.com. All rights reserved.

FIG 9.5 Photograph-Clark's Nutcracker, NPS Slides, NPS Digital Slides, Yellowstone by Jim Peaco, National Park Service, ©2012 under Creative Commons license.

FIG 9.6 Photograph-Whitebark Pine Trees, by Dave Powell, USDA Forest Service, ©2012 under Creative Commons license.

FIG 9.7 Photograph-Smog and Smoke, by Lindsay Douglas, ©2012, Used under license from Shutterstock.com. All rights reserved.

FIG 9.8 Photograph-Whitebark Pine Trees, by Robert L. Anderson, USDA Forest Service, ©2012 under Creative Commons license.

FIG 10.1 Illustration-Stockton Newspaper Caricature of Walter Fry, Walter Fry Family, Record 9-10-1925 by Ralph O. Yardley, ©2012 Provided with permission, All rights reserved.

FIG 10.2 Photograph-Tall Grass Prairie, Homestead National Monument, by Weldon Schloneger, ©2012, Used under license from Shutterstock.com. All rights reserved.

FIG 10.3 Photograph-Walter Fry, Age 16, provided by Fry Family, ©2012 with permission, All rights reserved.

FIG 10.4 Photograph-Two man Sawyers w/ ladder, woman against tree provided by NPS SEKI Archives, ©2012, All Rights Reserved

FIG 10.5 Graphic-Walter Fry Timeline, by C S Martin, ©2012 All rights reserved.

FIG 10.6 Photograph-Walter Fry on Horse with Dog, provided by Fry Family, ©2012 with permission, All rights reserved.

FIG 10.7 Photograph-Moro Rock, by Perri Martin, ©2012 All rights reserved.

FIG 10.8 Photograph-Pictographs, by Perri Martin, ©2012 All rights reserved.

FIG 10.9 Photograph-Pictographs up close, by Rick Webb, ©2012 All rights reserved.

FIG 10.10 Photograph-A view to outside, by Rick Webb, ©2012 All rights reserved.

FIG 10.11 Photograph-Fry with Grandson, Russel Weckert, provided by Fry Family, ©2012 with permission, All rights reserved.

Cover-Sequoia 1-10, layout and design by C S Martin; Photograph-Portrait of a Brown Bear by Andrey Ushakov Stock Free Images; Photograph-Grizzly Giant, Sequoia Tree taken Nov. 10, 2010 by Col Ford and Natasha de Vere, 2012 under Creative Commons license; Photograph-Sequoia and Kings Canyon National Parks Map by U.S. National Park Service (2012 version of map, NPS) [Public domain], via Wikimedia Commons

ACKNOWLEDGMENTS

Across the wide abyss of time, we take a moment to thank the first civilian superintendent of Sequoia National Park, Walter Fry, who recorded the journals, letters, photographs and bulletins that reveal the splendor of Sequoia's early days. Tucked away by great granddaughters, Joan Thomsen and Rachel Caggiano, these treasures were generously shared with this writer. The next generation of descendants, Perri Thomsen Martin and Rick Webb, provided outstanding current photos found throughout this book. Counted among the youngest progeny, Caden and Quinn Martin, and Jordan Webb devoted their time to spotting flora and fauna on our many hikes. We are grateful to all.

We express gratitude for the National Park Service, including the numerous park scientists, and rangers for their generous cooperation. Foremost among them is park curator, Ward Eldredge, obliging time and again with archival materials. Other accommodating contributors were Colleen Bathe, chief of interpretation, Danny Boiano, aquatic biologist, Joel Despain, park cave specialist, Athena Demetry, plant restoration ecologist, Danny Gammons, wildlife biologist, David Graber, chief scientist, Sylvia Haultain, plant ecologist, and Nate Stevenson, USGS research ecologist. Going the extra mile, William C. Tweed, park author and historian, is appreciated for his advice and early edits.

Scientist and children's author Caroline Hatton is cherished for her ever-ready expertise. We are indebted to the children's critique teams including Jean Castaing, Eloise Freeman, Juli Juteau, Julie "Rusty" Harris, Marci Hersel, Valerie Herzig, Carol Heyer, Mary-Jo Murphy, Linda Olson and Siri Weber Feeney. This book would not have seen the light of day without the expertise of Cindy Martin. My humble thanks.

Finally, with appreciation for Hank Weyand, who was always the wind beneath our wings and would have loved this outcome.

ABOUT THE AUTHOR
Mary Martin Weyand

It was the huge trees that towered above our little home in Nebraska that set the tone of my life. Curly-tailed squirrels scampered up tree trunks, while scolding me for chasing after them. At the ripe age of five, and tired of stalking, I'd tramp alone to the wooded area at the foot of our property. Fresh mint blanketed the ground, making an edible picnic cloth. I'd pick a bouquet, and contemplate what I'd do if a big old bear showed up. I wisely knew that I'd invite the bear for a cup of mint tea.

From that time forward, hiking up mountains, and through valleys, became my passion. The seduction of the American landscape, its natural wonders, and stories about America's brave inhabitants called me to write. But of course, practical needs, like putting food on the table, got in the way - for a time.

My professional work life began with newspaper publishing in Ventura County, California, and culminated with a twelve-year stint as owner of a California based marketing company. I sold my company and devoted time to produce Portraits of Success, an award-winning book I edited for Lupus International. Now, I've turned to my first love, writing for children. Picture books, poems and historic fiction stories have slipped from heart to keyboard. They are now followed by the latest, a non-fiction manuscript, Of Giants And Grizzlies.

FOR PURCHASING INFORMATION:

Of Giants and Grizzlies per chapter eBooks and/or additional copies can be easily purchased online via a web browser (i.e., Safari, Firefox, Chrome, IE, etc.)

Check us out at:
http://www.ofgiantsandgrizzlies.com/ebook-titles.html

MEET THE AUTHOR:
Mary Martin Weyand

http://www.marymartinweyand.com

NEW RELEASE NEWS:
To be one of the first to hear about my latest releases, sign up for the exclusive New Release News Mailing List:

http://www.marymartinweyand.com/getnewreleasenews.html

FREE FOR TEACHERS:
Of Giants and Grizzlies Curriculum guides are available for free in PDF format via a web browser (i.e., Safari, Firefox, Chrome, IE, etc.) at:

http://www.marymartinweyand.com/guides.html

Each per chapter guide reflects the Common Core Standards for the State of California.

Dear Reader,

To order additional Of Giants and Grizzlies books, signed by the author or to order signed books for gifts, please complete and return this form with payment to Write On For Kids, 348 Chestnut Hill Court, #21, Thousand Oaks, California, 91360. Or email at maryweyand1@gmail.com or call (805) 990-2082. Mary will sign each book, and return the entire order to you. Thank you!

BOOK ORDER & AUTOGRAPH FORM

Recipient Name(s) (please print, use back if needed) _____

_____

_____

_____

OF GIANTS AND GRIZZLIES _____ books @ $15 each* =

Total $_____ Please make check payable to:

WRITE ON FOR KIDS and return by mail.

*includes postage, USA only (Alaska, Hawaii, add $_____ for additional postage.) Outside of USA, postage added.

Your Name (please print) _____

Your Address:_____

City _____ State ____ Zip _____

Telephone _____ Email _____

Thanks for your order!